COOKING
FROM THE HIP

COOKING

FROM THE HIP

Olaf Mertens

whitecap

The information in this book is true and complete to the best of our knowledge. All recommendations
are made without guarantee on the part of the author or Whitecap Books Ltd. The author and publisher
disclaim any liability in connection with the use of this information. For additional information, please
contact Whitecap Books Ltd., 351 Lynn Avenue, North Vancouver, BC V7J 2C4

Edited by Kathy Evans
Proofread by Lesley Cameron
Interior design by Maxine Lea
Cover design by Tanya Lloyd Kyi/Spotlight Design
Cover and interior photographs by Christopher Freeland
Food styling by Olaf Mertens
Props supplied by Oksana Slavutych and Marc-Philippe Gagné

Printed and bound in Canada

National Library of Canada Cataloguing in Publication Data

Mertens, Olaf.
Cooking from the hip

Includes index.
ISBN 1-55285-335-7

1. Cookery. I.Title.
TX714.M46 2002   641.5   C2002-9100202-2

The publisher acknowledges the support of the Canada Council for the Arts and the Cultural Services
Branch of the Government of British Columbia for our publishing program. We acknowledge the financial
support of the Government of Canada through the Book Publishing Industry Development ΔProgram for
our publishing activities.

Table of Contents

Introduction

If you love to cook and you want to learn how trained chefs cook in a professional kitchen, then this is the book for you. People are always asking me, "How did you *do* that?" This book is intended to teach you how to cook in your own kitchen just like a professional chef. I've tried to avoid a lot of fancy cooking terms and exotic ingredients that might dampen your enthusiasm. All the ingredients are readily available in regular grocery stores or farmers' markets. My food has traditional methods and components, but it is given a fresh twist of imagination and simple contemporary presentation.

I am a passionate "foodie"! I love cooking, with all my heart and soul. I love to eat and drink and to share this passion with people who appreciate not only the food but also the effort involved in achieving gourmet feasts. Since my spare time is very limited, I always want to deliver a *wow* of a meal in as short a time as possible so I can spend more time with my guests. I define the Wow Factor as the taste, texture, surprises, presentation, and fun that a dish delivers. I hope that you catch my excitement and that, as you read through these pages, your first impulse is to grab your calendar to plan a day for inviting over a few friends so you can try out the recipes.

When I think about foods, recipes, or menus, I first consider flavors. Powerful flavors are achieved by aged, fully ripened, great raw ingredients. Slow roasting, stewing, or brewing ingredients marries their flavors together. Accenting flavors is done by adding natural sweeteners, acids, and salts. Every component on the plate should have a strong individual flavor, but, combined, the ingredients should complement one another and excite the taste buds. Another consideration is texture! How to excite the senses while eating crispy, crunchy, creamy, moist, light, fluffy, hot, and cold textures? Basically I strive to satisfy all the taste buds and senses.

Also important for satisfying your senses is presentation, since your eyes eat along with you. I use a few components on a plate. It isn't necessary to overwork the plate with presentation and flavors . . . try to keep it simple!

My grade-school years were spent in my parents' European deli and specialty food store. That time, combined with my summers in Germany with my grandparents, led me to my passion for cooking. I realize now that they too were "foodies." I remember those summer days being planned around eating meals of regional and traditional cuisine. I still remember trips to the market and stirring pots in my grandparents' kitchens, always watching and wanting to learn. I became hooked on cooking and, by 14 years of age, I was duplicating recipes with great success. It was then that I realized I desperately wanted to become a *chef*!

By the time I completed high school, I was already catering a few small events. I got myself started at Mississauga, Ontario's, finest restaurant, *Rogues Restaurant*. I started as a dishwasher, but within a week Carlos Perfetti, the chef/owner, saw my desire to learn and immediately put me to work in the "cold kitchen" making salads and desserts. As I learned, my confidence and enthusiasm grew.

Being a German citizen gave me a unique opportunity to qualify for one of Germany's aprenticeship programs. My grandfather's contacts were able to get me into the Steigenberger Hotel as an 18-year-old apprentice. One of the largest five-star hotel chains in Germany, the hotel had huge kitchens and several respected master chefs on staff. I set about learning European traditions, skill requirements, and, of course, the utmost discipline. Four days a week at the hotel, two days a week at school, and a couple of shifts a week at a little Swedish restaurant for extra money—I was very busy but I was on my way!

I returned to Canada after three dream years, hard as they were, as a young, eager chef ready to take on any kitchen that would have me. My dear friend and mentor, Chef Carlos Perfetti, again offered me a position in his establishment, this time as sous chef. I was far too young for the position, but I accepted his offer and took on the challenge. Carlos took over where Germany left off— educating me about life, about how to treat people, about business, and, of course, about food. He continued to consolidate my culinary abilities by teaching me the basics of Italian cooking and the importance of freshness, quality, touch, smell, and sight. He also introduced me to the reality of the kitchen as a business, not just a playground. He taught things like, "You can cook with all the best ingredients, but if it's too expensive, no one will buy it"—those lessons, in time, would prove to be indispensable.

After several years of the fine-dining "grind," I felt it was time to return to Germany to go back to school. I enrolled in the world-renowned Steigenberger Hotel School and cooked my way to a Kuchenmeister—a Master Chef's degree. This six-month program, condensed into three intense months, meant leaving my position as head chef at *Rogues*, as well as leaving my wife and nine-month-old son at home. It was a huge decision.

The months in the picturesque southern Bavarian Alps gave me an opportunity to meet chefs from all over Germany. I not only made—and kept—some very good friends, I also had the opportunity to cook in some great kitchens. Bavarian regional gourmet cooking—fabulous!

Eventually my path led me to Brian Meikle in Toronto. And then came the HIP, an acronym for Hospitality-Inspired People, also based in Toronto. It's the hospitality team of the millennium: Brian, Mike Wilson, and myself. We each have our hospitality specialties, and are well-supported by our wives, Lily Meikle, Teresa Wilson, and my wife, Jennifer; and we all play a strong role in the everyday running and future design of the HIP Restaurants. The HIP kitchens are my creative playground to teach, to master new ideas, to update old concepts, and of course, to share it all with our customers.

The recipes in this book are the result of my Germanic classic training and techniques being combined with my own "twists." My goal was to present the recipes to you in simple cooking styles that emphasize flavor and taste. They are not all easy recipes. I try to show that the difference between "dinner" and "magic" is in the extra details—homemade stocks, an extra-special sauce, or an extraordinary presentation. I've included a few culinary tips and short cuts to achieve the best results in the shortest time possible.

I love to get up every morning because it's such a privilege to get into my kitchens to be creative and indulge my passion each and every day! I now invite you to join me—let me take you on a culinary odyssey. Read on and remember the Wow Factors—taste, texture, surprises, presentation and above all fun! Enjoy cooking with a twist!

This book is dedicated to food lovers—the passionate people who grow it, cook it, and really appreciate it. Food can be just a matter of nutrition, but a meal should not be just a meal. It should be a special time, a time when we slow down, enjoy flavors, friendships, and conversation. Food lovers know and appreciate that the world revolves around food!

The book is also dedicated:

To my grandparents, Oma Hausner and Oma Pfaff and especially my Opa Pfaff. They were passionate about preparing good food and drink. They passed down to us an appreciation for quality foods and German traditions. They also made possible my apprenticeship and my education in the technical and practical preparation of food in Germany.

To my parents, Marion and Bernd. They divorced when I was young, and this forced my father, brother and myself to learn to cook for ourselves, starting with the basics. The time with my mom gave me a new appreciation for food and meal times because my mom worked such long hours. My brother and I had to fend for ourselves for meals, so I learned to cook by trial and error. Sundays were our day together so I would grocery-shop and prepare a meal for the three of us. What we ate was less important than the realization that dinner time was a great way to stay connected to one another.

To my loving wife, Jennifer, whom I met in high school and who was taken in by my passion for food—and who continues to love me in spite of this sometimes all-consuming passion. She gives me her love and support, and I thank her for being by my side as I made the trek from "dishwasher" to "chef de cuisine." She has kept me focused and is certainly one of my greatest critics. We have learned together that really good dining is food that has magic. She makes sure mine has!

To my three sons, Nicolas, Taylor, and Owen, my assistant junior chefs, who have kept me on my toes and taught me the fine art of pizza- and cookie-making. The real magic happens when I am at home with my family, where we too try to teach that dinner together is an event to be cherished.

Finally, to all the young chefs who have discovered the excitement of gastronomy. "Cook from the heart," I say, and put passion on every plate. Enjoy using this book as much as I enjoyed writing it.

Acknowledgments

With great food comes great family, friends, and colleagues, and food has certainly brought me closer to all of these special people. I want to thank some especially.

To Donna "Mrs. U" Urquhart: many thanks to my long-time fan, supporter, mother-in-law, and co-writer.

To Gary, Marty, Louise, Alison, Chris, Leah, and Jade, my family and Sunday-dinner taste-testers: thanks for your support and for washing all those years' worth of dishes.

To Robert McCullough and Alison Maclean at Whitecap Books: for making one of my all-time dreams come true, thank you is not enough.

To Chris Freeland and Tracy Cox: you make my food come to life with your mouth-watering, edible photographs.

To Chef Ryan Skelton: *you* can cook the magic!

To Chef Luther Miller: a true Canadian crazy *garde manger*—keep whisking!

To Ted Reader: bigger than life itself! You want passion, imagination, flavor? This is the man. Thanks for so much, Big Buddha!

To Brian Meikle: my friend, partner, true supporter, and dessert connoisseur. Thanks also to Mike and Teresa Wilson: friends, partners, and foodies in the true spirit of the word.

To the HIP Restaurants team members: a real big thanks. All my chefs, cooks, dishwashers, bartenders, servers, busboys, and everyone else who together help make our guests' visits a truly special event every time. You give me motivation, keep me fresh and in touch, and help me to push the envelope.

To Buddha Michael and Anna Olson: friends, fellow chefs, and advisors—so many, many thanks.

To Chef Dale McCarthy: the Serious Chef, Mr. Detail. Thanks, and remember to embrace the German beer bitters!

To Carlos, Tony, Bevan, Pascal, Joe, Luis, Philip, Petra, Stefan, Raza, Maggie, and everyone at *Rogues Restaurant*: it was a wonderful time. Lessons for a lifetime.

To my German culinary influences and friends: Bernd Siener and his family at his Backery Siener in Mainz. Stefan and the Zipf family at Weissen Ross in Grossheubach and Otto and Uli Bachmaier in Bavaria. You have been there from the beginning.

To my associates at Humber College: Robert, Michael, Tony, Frank, Klaus, and Jürgen. Passing on the passion was a privilege.

And finally: a really big thank you to all my friends and regular customers.

Foreword

Chef Olaf Mertens: One German Master Chef's Culinary Experience

Dear Readers,

It is my pleasure to introduce you to a wonderful friend, colleague, and chef, Olaf Mertens.

I first met Olaf, also known as Oli Canoli, Oooodle Canooooodle, and Baby Buddha, in the spring of 1996 when I was invited to join the Team Canada culinary team on a journey to Southern Ireland to compete in the Epicurean World Master Chefs' Society international banqueting competition. Olaf was our team captain, our leader on a culinary experience unlike any I had ever had. As a team of 15 we made our journey to Southern Ireland where we worked, played, and cooked hard—and consumed half of the Guinness in the country. Olaf led us to a silver medal, just narrowly beaten by a competitive U.S. team. We had the experience of a lifetime.

Olaf brings a new style of cuisine to the Toronto area, where he blends his culinary passions of Germany with the flavors of the world. Classically trained, Olaf is one of the few true Master Chefs in North America—an elite group of culinary masters who have trained and studied the culinary arts with intensity and a desire to be the best in all areas of the kitchen.

Olaf has worked in many areas of the culinary arts and has achieved great success and a following for his wonderful food. From his days working the stoves as chef for *Rogues Restaurant* in Mississauga, Ontario, to being the corporate chef of a ten-plus restaurant chain, to finally owning his own restaurants and catering company, he is dedicated to preparing the best-tasting dishes with flavors from around the world. He makes mouth-watering pan-seared Atlantic salmon, and his foie gras terrine is to kill for, according to my wonderful wife Pamela. When Olaf makes foie gras it is delicious, and I only wish that I could prepare it as well. Olaf's touch with food is like butter—smooth and rich and truly a necessity for any great dish.

I have had the pleasure of traveling to many places with Olaf and our other chef friends. We have cooked in the bayous of Louisiana, toured the vineyards and beer gardens of Germany, had succulent barbecues in Texas, and have spent many hours cooking together over some very hot stoves. I have learned a great deal from my friend Olaf and feel that I have become a better chef from his teachings.

Olaf has a real dedication to teaching others the culinary arts. He spends many hours teaching at Humber College in Toronto, and also gives private cooking classes. He is always willing to lend a hand to new culinary engineers and even those of us who sometimes run out of time and need a few emergency dishes for a last-minute catering function. Olaf's food can be measured by his passion for cooking, whether it be simply burgers or his famous schnitzel or a roast suckling pig.

So when you visit one of Olaf's fine restaurants, make sure to rub Olaf's belly for good luck.

Prosit, and Embrace the Bitter,

Ted Reader, *King of the Q*

Getting Started

Basics

This section presents the key basics you will need for preparing many of the recipes in this book. They are the bones to the body of the great dishes that follow. Some of these preparations, such as those for the rich stocks, take a little time, but they are the flavor-enhancing power behind many of the dishes. Other recipes, such as the HIP Restaurants signature dressings, are much quicker to prepare but still provide the punch to many salads.

The "basics" can be made a couple of days before the dining event to make preparation day easier. And most of these recipes are great for freezing or refrigerating, for use in other meal preparations. There is no better way to boost the flavor of a quick rice dish than to cook it in one of your own homemade stocks.

I recommend that you give these basics a try because they have a strong structure, achieved by being homemade; however, faint-of-heart or rushed cooks can use pre-made convenience products available in good grocery stores. I suggest substitutions in "Olaf's Tips."

Dressings

These vinaigrettes are the signature dressings in all the HIP Restaurants in Toronto. A basic rule for making a vinaigrette is to use one part acid (vinegar, lemon, etc.) to three or four parts body (oils, water, or stock). Vegetable oils are preferred so as not to overpower the dominant flavor of the dressing. I use olive oil sparingly and more as a flavor enhancer in stronger-tasting recipes, so that it doesn't overwhelm the other flavors. Using vegetable or canola-type oils will not only lighten the flavor but also reduce the fat/calorie content.

You will notice that in some recipes I have suggested using vegetable stock or water rather than oil. This helps lighten the fat content and the actual weight on the salad itself. You can find the recipe for vegetable stock on page 23, or you can buy a pre-made product from your grocery store.

Buy the good olive oil and balsamic vinegars, as their quality will dramatically alter the quality of flavors in your dressing.

For a change, pick up a different ingredient for your salads, or top them with additions such as roasted pumpkin seeds, shaved or grated cheeses, or vine-ripened tomatoes—the choices are endless.

Caesar Vinaigrette

Makes about 5 cups (1.2 L)

This is the Caesar dressing for the lighter of heart: no heavy egg or mayonnaise taste. Just a lot of strong flavors lightly coating crispy leaves.

10	cloves garlic, roasted (see Tip)	10
¼ cup	Dijon mustard	60 mL
¾ cup	white wine vinegar	180 mL
¼ cup	anchovies, drained	60 mL
¼ cup	capers, drained	60 mL
1	lemon, juice of	1
1 tsp.	Worcestershire sauce	5 mL
½ tsp.	hot pepper sauce	2.5 mL
4 cups	vegetable or olive oil	960 mL
	salt and white pepper to taste	

In a food processor, blender, or with a hand whisk, mix all ingredients, except the oil, salt, and pepper. Blend to make a smooth mixture. While still mixing, drizzle in the oil very slowly. When all the oil has been added, stop to taste. Season and blend one more time. Keeps in refrigerator for up to 7 days. Reblend or whisk before each use.

Olaf's Tip: I like to roast my garlic for this recipe to bring out every possible flavor of this amazing staple. One way to roast garlic is to take the whole garlic bulb, place on a piece of tin foil, sprinkle with some olive oil, and tightly wrap the bulb in the foil. Bake at 350°F (175°C) for 20 minutes. Carefully open the foil, remove the bulb, and squeeze out the creamy garlic from each clove. Or you can take about a third of the oil from the recipe, and roast the peeled garlic cloves in it until lightly browned. Cool and continue with the recipe. This vinaigrette has a slight tartness, which some people prefer, but can be adjusted to your particular liking by reducing the vinegar amount. Using olive oil makes this dressing just that much more flavorful. You can use the full amount of either oil or half of each to reduce the strong olive oil flavor.

Citrus Vinaigrette

Makes about 5 cups (1.2 L)

Fresh citrus juices made into a quick vinaigrette—a great fruity acid to start a menu. This acidic start to a meal gets the stomach excited, ready to receive the delights to come.

2 cups	orange juice	480 mL
4	lemons, juice of	4
3	limes, juice of	3
½ cup	white wine vinegar	120 mL
½ cup	liquid honey	120 mL
½ cup	vegetable stock or water	120 mL
½ cup	vegetable oil	120 mL
	salt and white pepper to taste	

Place all ingredients into a food processor or blender and mix for 2 minutes. Stop to adjust seasonings and blend for 30 seconds. Keeps in the refrigerator for up to 7 days. Reblend or whisk before each use.

 Olaf's Tip: I use real lemons and limes for this recipe. If you are using the bottled juices, check the bottle for measurements to coincide with these amounts. Lemons and limes produce more juice and are easier to extract the juice from if they are at room temperature. If still cold, briefly microwave the fruit and roll on the counter with the palm of your hand before juicing. You will notice a big difference.

Honey Balsamic Vinaigrette

Makes about 5 cups (1.2 L)

This is the most versatile vinaigrette; great for salads, grilled meats, fish, and tossed vegetables. Make a big batch because it won't last long.

1 cup	balsamic vinegar	240 mL
½ cup	finely chopped shallots or a small onion	120 mL
¼ cup	Dijon mustard	60 mL
2	lemons, juice of	2
½ cup	liquid honey	120 mL
1 tsp.	fresh thyme	5 mL
1 tsp.	fresh oregano	5 mL
3 cups	vegetable oil	720 mL
	salt and pepper to taste	

In a food processor or blender, mix all the ingredients, except the oil, salt, and pepper. When completely smooth, and while still mixing, slowly drizzle in the oil. Stop and adjust seasonings. Blend for another 30 seconds. Keeps in the refrigerator for up to 7 days.

 Olaf's Tip: For a more refined dressing, let the dressing sit for at least 24 hours to let the flavors really blend. Use a fine strainer to remove the little "bits" of herbs and onions. You will end up with a velvety-smooth glaze for your salad.

Stocks

Having good stocks is crucial. They are the very backbone of a good kitchen pantry. There are so many uses for stocks—soups, dressings, sauces, pasta, risotto—that you can never have enough. Stored in little tubs or ice cube trays, they speed up a quick dinner or the preparation time of a dinner-party menu. Some important things to remember when making a good, clear, flavorful and powerful stock:

1. Use ice cubes and cold water.

2. Simmer slowly at low temperature.

3. Skim and discard residue and fat carefully and often.

4. Do not stir the pot.

5. Be patient. It takes time—lots of it! It's not something to make the day you need it; it's something to put on the back burner, make a large amount, and freeze.

6. Ladle out the broth from the pot very carefully to ensure a clear broth.

7. Stocks can be stored in the refrigerator for one week or stored in the freezer for one month.

8. Freeze the stock in small containers or ice cube trays, then pop them into a marked plastic bag.

Fish Stock

Makes about 4 cups (1 L)

This flavorful stock is the start of any great seafood soup, chowder, sauce, or light broth to accompany a medley of seafood.

1	large onion, finely diced	1
4	stalks celery, finely diced	4
1	leek, white only, finely diced	1
1	bulb fennel, finely diced	1
1 cup	quartered mushroom	240 mL
4 cups	cold water	960 mL
2 lbs.	fish bones	900 g
2 cups	white wine	480 mL
4 cups	ice cubes	960 mL
2	bay leaves	2
1 Tbsp.	cracked white peppercorns	15 mL
2 Tbsp.	sea salt	30 mL

Place all vegetables in a stockpot or other large, heavy-bottomed pot, then add the cold water, fish bones, white wine, and ice cubes. Slowly bring to a simmer to remove any residue and fat that will rise to the surface. With a spoon, skim this off and discard. Important in making a good stock: do not stir the pot!

Once at a simmer, add the seasonings and continue simmering uncovered for 45 minutes. Remove from heat and, with a ladle or by pouring very carefully, remove the stock without disturbing the bones. Quickly chill. This stock can be frozen in small tubs or in ice cube trays for future use.

Olaf's Tip: Use lean fish bones from white fish; for example, snapper, halibut, or flounder. Some fish bones, like salmon's, tend to be very oily. To ensure a clear broth, remove any bits of the cut-up fish by rinsing all the bones in cold water before using.

Chicken Stock

Makes 8 cups (2 L)

A great strong-flavored chicken stock is halfway to a great dish. A mug of this stock is a remedy to ward off the start of a cold.

6 lbs.	chicken leg quarters, bones in	2.7 kg
8 cups	cold water	2 L
10 cups	ice cubes	2.4 L
2	medium onions, chopped	2
4	stalks celery, chopped	4
1	sprig fresh thyme	1
1	bay leaf	1
1 Tbsp.	cracked white peppercorns	15 mL
4	sprigs parsley	4

Place chicken quarters into a stockpot or other large, heavy-bottomed pot and cover with cold water and ice cubes. Bring slowly to a simmer. As the stock warms, residue and fat will come to the surface. Using a spoon, gently skim this off and discard. Do not stir the pot!

Once the stock reaches a simmer, add the remaining ingredients and continue to simmer, uncovered, for 3 hours, skimming regularly. The longer the stock simmers, the better the flavor will be.

Carefully ladle the clear stock out of the pot. Do not pour the stock quickly, to avoid a cloudy, unpure broth. Chill the stock quickly to avoid any contamination by placing in a larger container of ice cubes.

Duck Stock

Makes 8 cups (2 L)

I use this wonder stock in Duck Orange Punch on page 72.

2 lbs.	duck leg quarters and bones	900 g
½ cup	vegetable oil	120 mL
1 Tbsp.	salt	15 mL
2	stalks celery, diced	2
1	large onion, diced	1
1	large tomato, diced	1
1 Tbsp.	tomato paste	15 mL
1 cup	Madeira wine	240 mL
2 cups	red wine	480 mL
16 cups	cold water	4 L
8 cups	ice cubes	2 L
1	sprig fresh rosemary	1
1	sprig fresh thyme	1
2	bay leaves	2
1 Tbsp.	black peppercorns	15 mL
	salt and pepper to taste	

In a stockpot or other large, heavy-bottomed pot on medium-high heat, season the duck legs and bones with salt and roast in oil for 5–10 minutes. Add the vegetables and roast until golden brown. Add the tomato paste and continue roasting until brown. Add the Madeira wine, reduce by 90% or for approximately 10 minutes, add the red wine, reduce by 90% or for approximately 15 minutes. Finally, add the cold water and ice cubes and simmer uncovered for 3 hours. During the last half hour, toss in the herbs and seasonings. Strain the broth carefully, ladle by ladle, into a clean container. Chill the stock quickly to avoid any contamination by placing in a larger container of ice cubes.

Makes 8 cups (2 L)

This stock is invaluable for vegetarian dishes and soups, as well as a great way to lighten up salad dressings by reducing the oil and using this stock instead. Keeping this stock in ice cube trays is a definite advantage for easy, quick dressings.

1 cup	unsalted butter	240 mL
3	carrots, diced	3
3	onions, diced	3
1	bulb fennel, diced	1
2	leeks, white only, sliced	2
2	tomatoes, diced	2
10 cups	cold water	2.4 L
10 cups	ice cubes	2.4 L
1	bundle fresh parsley	1
1	bundle fresh basil	1
2	sprigs fresh thyme	2
2	cloves garlic, whole	2
1 Tbsp.	cracked black peppercorns	15 mL
1	bay leaf	1
1½ Tbsp.	salt	22.5 mL
1 tsp.	white pepper	5 mL

In a stockpot or other large, heavy-bottomed pot on medium heat, melt the butter and sweat off the vegetables and garlic for about 10 minutes or until light brown. Add the cold water and ice cubes and reduce the temperature to medium. Simmer uncovered for 2 hours. During the last half hour, add the herbs and seasonings. Strain the broth carefully, ladle by ladle, into a clean container. Chill the stock quickly to avoid any contamination by placing in a larger container of ice cubes.

 Olaf's Tip: With a piece of string, tie the fresh herb sprigs together and add to the broth in the last half hour to ensure that the fresh fragrances remain strong.

Court Bouillon

Makes 4 cups (1 L)

A court bouillon is a super-strong flavor enhancer, usually used to poach fish or seafood in. I use this court bouillon in Wacky, Tacky Shrimp Cocktail, page 60.

6 cups	water	1.5 L
½ cup	vinegar	120 mL
3 Tbsp.	salt	45 mL
1	lemon, juice and zest of	1
1 cup	diced onions	240 mL
½ cup	diced carrot	120 mL
2	sprigs fresh thyme	2
3	bay leaves	3
¼ cup	chopped fresh parsley	60 mL
1 Tbsp.	cracked white peppercorns	15 mL

Simmer all ingredients except the peppercorns for about 30 minutes. Add the peppercorns and continue to simmer for another 10 minutes. Taste and adjust seasonings to make sure this strong flavor-booster will add some punch to your seafood or fish dish. Strain the broth carefully, ladle by ladle, into a clean container. Chill the stock quickly to avoid any contamination by placing in a larger container of ice cubes. Store in the refrigerator for 3 days or freeze in containers or ice cube trays.

 Olaf's Tip: After poaching, chill the fish, the seafood, and the bouillon together to get extra flavor and moisture. Chill for as long as 24 hours.

Sauces

Sauces are the finishing touch to any dish, savory or sweet. A sauce is used to give a dish texture, to enhance the flavors, or to give some flavor contrast. A sauce can also give moisture to the dish and marry many flavors together. The following sauces have so many uses—I've given you some ideas, but don't be afraid to use them on some of your own favorite dishes.

Sauces should be heated to a low simmer and should be the finishing touch to a perfectly prepared piece of meat or fish. The sauce can be poured on the plate first and the meat or fish placed on top. Or, you can top the meat or fish with the sauce but only on half of it, so you show some contrast in colors.

Save the extra sauces in small containers or in ice cube trays. These frozen cubes, explosive with flavor, will save a lot of time for those rushed dinners and will make you look like a great cook in a short period of preparation time.

White Wine and Lemon Butter Sauce

Makes 1 cup (240 mL)

This sauce creates one of my wife's favorite smells in the kitchen. It's great with chicken, veal, or pork. In this book, I use it in Surf and Turf Wellington, page 122, and a variation of it with Arctic Char on Mussels Citrus Stew, page 110.

¼ cup	unsalted butter	60 mL
6	shallots, diced or 1 small white onion, diced	6
2 cups	white wine	480 mL
1	bay leaf	1
2	lemons, juice and zest of	2
⅓ cup	35% cream	80 mL
1 cup	cold unsalted butter, cubed	240 mL
	salt and white pepper to taste	

In a small pot on medium heat, melt ¼ cup (60 mL) of butter and sweat off the shallots or onion. Add the white wine, bay leaf, lemon juice and zest and reduce by 90% or until no liquid remains. Add the cream and reduce by 90% until large bubbles appear. Remove from heat and whisk, gradually adding all the cold butter cubes. Strain the mixture through a fine mesh strainer into a new small container and season.

Basil Cream Sauce

Makes 1 cup (240 mL)

This is a rich, creamy version of a wine sauce that I use in my Surf and Turf Wellington, page 122, but can also be great with fish or as the body to a shellfish pasta.

1	sprig fresh basil	1
¼ cup	unsalted butter	60 mL
6	shallots, finely diced or 1 small white onion, finely diced	6
1 cup	white wine	240 mL
1	bay leaf	1
1 cup	35% cream	240 mL
½ cup	35% cream, whipped	120 mL
	salt and white pepper to taste	

Cut 6 basil leaves into fine strips and set them aside. Melt the butter in a small pot on medium heat and sauté the shallots or onion until translucent. Deglaze with the white wine and add the remaining basil and the bay leaf. Reduce by 80% and add the one cup of cream. Simmer for 5 minutes at medium temperature until reduced by 25% of the volume. Season and strain through a fine mesh strainer into a clean saucepan. Bring to a simmer and, just before serving, stir in the finely sliced basil and fold in the whipped cream.

Vanilla Cream Sauce
or Crème Anglaise

Makes 2 cups (480 mL)

This is a wonderful accompaniment to any dessert. Since it is a delicate sauce, it needs to be tempered. By this I mean you slowly pour a small amount of the warmed cream into the cold egg mixture and mix well and quickly, then gradually add the rest of the warmed cream so that the eggs don't cook or scramble. It sounds tricky but is well worth the effort.

1½ cups	10% cream	360 mL
1	vanilla bean, split and scraped	1
¼ cup	sugar	60 mL
6	large egg yolks	6
¼ cup	sugar	60 mL
½ cup	10% cream	120 mL
½ tsp.	salt	2.5 mL

Combine the 1½ cups (360 mL) of cream, the vanilla bean, and ¼ cup (60 mL) sugar in a pot on the stove. Bring to a simmer, uncovered, and remove from the heat. Let sit for 15 minutes. In a stainless steel bowl, combine the egg yolks, the ¼ cup (60 mL) sugar, and the ½ cup (120 mL) of cream until smooth. Slowly temper the cream mixture into the egg mixture and gently cook over a double boiler while whisking constantly. Cook until the custard coats the back of a spoon, approximately 10–15 minutes. Strain through a fine mesh strainer into a clean container and quickly chill.

 Olaf's Tip: This sauce can also be used as an ice cream by pouring the chilled mixture into a home ice cream maker and following the manufacturer's instructions.

Makes about 2 cups (480 mL)

A twist on a regular chocolate sauce, with the addition of honey and sour cream to give it a rich and silky consistency. It has so many uses! In Mandarin Sticky Cake, page 194, this sauce makes the tangy orange cake something really special. Use it for an ice cream topping, in a milk drink, or to dress up any dessert.

1 cup	35% cream	240 mL
¼ cup	honey	60 mL
2 Tbsp.	unsalted butter	30 mL
8 oz.	semi-sweet chocolate, finely chopped	225 g
3 Tbsp.	sour cream	45 mL

In a small pot on medium heat, add the cream, honey, and butter together. Add the chopped chocolate. When completely melted, stir in the sour cream. Keep at room temperature for serving. Will keep well in the refrigerator for 3 days.

 Olaf's Tip: After storing in the refrigerator, the sauce must be slowly reheated before the next use.

Raspberry Coulis

Makes about 2 cups (480 mL)

A very useful recipe: it is a great topper for ice cream, or you can blend in whole berries for a summer berry stew, or, like many chefs do, set a simple dessert on a pool of this sauce to really make an impression.

½ cup	icing sugar	120 mL
1	lemon, juice of	1
2 cups	water	480 mL
1 pint (2 cups)	raspberries	480 mL

Combine icing sugar, lemon juice, and water in a pot over medium heat. Bring to a simmer until the liquid is a syrup-like consistency. Add the raspberries and simmer 5 minutes. Remove from the heat and purée using a blender or hand blender, then strain through a fine mesh strainer. Cool completely and store in the refrigerator for up to 3 days. May be frozen for longer storage.

Herb Mayonnaise

Makes about 3 cups (720 mL)

I've taken a basic mayonnaise and "put it on the top shelf." Gives a finishing touch to fish, but is especially great as a sandwich or burger spread.

2 cups	mayonnaise	480 mL
½ cup	chopped fresh parsley	120 mL
¼ cup	chopped fresh tarragon	60 mL
½ cup	chopped fresh chives	120 mL
1 tsp.	paprika	5 mL
1	lemon, juice of	1
dash	Worcestershire sauce	dash
	salt and white pepper to taste	

Make this ahead of time. Combine all ingredients and refrigerate to bring the flavors together. Stores well in the refrigerator for 2–3 days.

 Olaf's Tip: Use low-fat mayonnaise or plain yogurt to reduce the fat content.

Tempura Batter

Makes about 4 cups (1 L)

This amazing batter can be used for many recipes. I use it for the Seafood Tempura Skewers, page 39. Try making fresh onion rings with it, using Vidalia or Spanish onions. A really impressive, easy idea is to dip fresh cooking apples in this batter, cook, and serve with ice cream as a dessert.

1 cup	corn starch	240 mL
1 cup	flour	240 mL
2 tsp.	salt	10 mL
1 tsp.	cayenne pepper	5 mL
1 tsp.	sesame seed oil	5 mL
¾ cup	ice-cold carbonated water	180 mL
½ cup	white wine	120 mL

Place all dry ingredients into a bowl and lightly whisk until blended. Continue whisking and slowly add the oil, water, and wine until smooth. Let rest for 15 minutes. Place the mixing bowl in a bowl of ice to keep the batter well chilled until ready to use.

 Olaf's Tip: The ice-cold carbonated water will help to achieve a light, crispy batter.

Lemon Cream Dip

Makes 1½ cups (360 mL)

This is a tangy, thick, and creamy dipping sauce, great with seafood, smoked fish, or chicken. I've matched it with Seafood Tempura Skewers, page 39, as well as Potato Skins for Grown-ups, page 40.

1 cup	sour cream	240 mL
¼ cup	lemon juice	60 mL
½ cup	chopped fresh chives	120 mL
¼ cup	grainy mustard	60 mL
	salt and white pepper to taste	

Mix all ingredients together. Stores in the refrigerator for 3–4 days.

Schupfnudeln
(Potato Finger Noodles)

Makes 12 fingers, about 3 inches (7.5 cm) long

This is my German twist on the Italian gnocchi dumpling. Like kids' play clay, this hand-rolled dough is roughly formed into a long tube shape. A unique, light starch accompaniment and great for dishes with lots of sauce. I've used it with my Roast Duckling with Grapefruit and Peppercorn Glaze, page 138.

3	medium Yukon Gold or russet potatoes	3
2/3 cup	flour	160 mL
1	large egg	1
pinch	salt	pinch
1 tsp.	white pepper	5 mL
1/2 tsp.	nutmeg	2.5 mL
2 Tbsp.	unsalted butter	30 mL

In a small pot, cook the potatoes, skin on, until fork-tender, then drain well. While still warm, peel the potatoes and press through a ricer to a fine purée. Place mixture into a bowl and quickly fold in the flour, egg, salt, pepper, and nutmeg. Portion into ¼-cup (60-mL) balls and roll the balls between the palms of your hands into finger-shaped tubes. Allow to chill completely. Blanch in salted boiling water for 2 minutes and strain. Heat the butter in a non-stick pan and lightly brown the noodles for one minute per side.

B-52 Tomato Shooters with Raw Oysters (page 48)

Cashew-Crusted Scallops with Asian Vegetable Salad (page 58)

Chicken Fricassée (page 94)

Roast Chicken Breast Supreme with Shrimp Stuffing (page 134)

Arctic Char on Mussel Citrus Stew (page 110)

Atlantic Salmon with Onions[3] (page 101)

New Age Fish and Chips with A Chunky Citrus Tartar Sauce (page 106)

Surf and Turf Wellington (page 122)

Makes 1 cup (240 mL)

Think of the brown sugar-type crumble used on apple or peach desserts. This is the same idea, but it's a savory flavor to be used on meats or fish. I love this on a grilled pork loin steak, but it is equally good on a fish fillet. Cook your meat or fish, then add a new dimension by topping it with this crumble. It adds a crunchy herb texture and interest to simple meals.

½ cup	unsalted butter, room temperature	120 mL
¼ cup	fresh white bread crumbs*	60 mL
1	clove garlic, minced	1
1 Tbsp.	Parmesan cheese	15 mL
	salt and black pepper to taste	
1 Tbsp.	chopped fresh rosemary	15 mL
1 Tbsp.	chopped fresh thyme	15 mL
1 cup	parsley	240 mL

*See Glossary, page 202.

Combine all ingredients together and knead to make a dough. Keep at room temperature before using. Crumble over top of meats or fish in the last 5 minutes of baking. Adds a great texture to any meat dish.

 Olaf's Tip: To ensure that the crust is not too dry, use stale white bread with the crusts removed to make the crumbs. I find that a day-old French loaf is very nice. Try not to use commercial bread crumbs as they will make the crust quite dry since they absorb a lot of moisture. It is very important to wash, rinse, and dry the parsley before using or the crust will turn green.

Crispy Flatbread

Makes four 8- x 12-inch (20-cm x 30-cm) sheets

A great addition to a modern bread basket or a perfect savory wafer to be used to scoop any of my great party-snack dips while "Cocktailing."

2 cups	all-purpose flour	480 mL
1 tsp.	sugar	5 mL
½ tsp.	salt	2.5 mL
4	large eggs, whites only	4
1 Tbsp.	olive oil	15 mL
½ cup	warm water	120 mL

For egg wash:

| 1 | large egg | 1 |
| ½ cup | milk | 120 mL |

Topping suggestions:

Spices: chili powder, cumin, caraway, sea salt

Herbs: freshly chopped rosemary, oregano, thyme

Nuts: pine nuts, walnuts, hazelnuts, sunflower seeds, green pumpkin seeds

Other: sliced olives, sun-dried tomatoes, thin slices of red pepper

Preheat the oven to 400°F (200°C). Using a mixer with a bread paddle, mix the flour, sugar, and salt. In a separate bowl, combine the egg whites, olive oil, and warm water and slowly add into the flour mixture. Wrap the dough in plastic wrap and let it rest in the refrigerator for about half an hour. Roll out to ⅛-inch (.3 cm), cut into shapes such as triangles or rectangles, and place on a baking sheet. Glaze with the egg wash and top with your choice of toppings. Bake 8 minutes.

 Olaf's Tip: For a rustic look, make the sheets as large as the recipe allows for and after baking, break into large pieces and place in a bread basket.

Makes about 16 medium or 24 small crepes

This recipe is used to make my "Spaghetti and Meatballs" dessert on page 198 for a "grand finale" to a meal. Leave out the sugar and vanilla to use as a brunch, lunch, or appetizer item. Use your imagination with the fillings to add a real twist to this classic.

2 Tbsp.	sugar	30 mL
½ tsp.	salt	2.5 mL
½ cup	flour	120 mL
⅓ cup	unsalted butter, melted	80 mL
1¼ cups	milk	300 mL
2	large eggs	2
½ tsp.	vanilla extract	2.5 mL

In a bowl, toss the dry ingredients. In a separate bowl, combine the butter, milk, eggs, and vanilla. Whisk in the dry ingredients. Strain through a fine mesh strainer, cover with a clean cloth, and let rest for 30 minutes before making crepes.

 Olaf's Tip: Use the crepes with fresh seasonal berries, crème fraîche, whipped cream, and a mint leaf—there are so many variations. Double the recipe and freeze some to have on hand for a quick dessert.

Strudel Dough

Makes one 3-foot- (90-cm-) long log of strudel!

For a different twist, this strudel dough can be used with garden vegetables, as in Vegetable Strudel, page 152. This light, crisp dough is the base for a wonderful sweet or savory creation—just set your creativity free!

1⅓ cups	flour	320 mL
½ tsp.	salt	2.5 mL
⅔ cup	warm water	160 mL
¼ cup	vegetable oil	60 mL

Combine the flour and salt and make a well in the middle. Carefully, with your hands, work in the water and oil to form a soft dough. Let rest for 30 minutes.

Preheat the oven to 350°F (175°C). Using a table or large surface, covered with a clean cloth and floured, roll out the dough ¼-inch (.6-cm) thick. With your hands, start evenly stretching the dough until paper-thin while circling the table. This part is much easier if you have someone to help. You should be able to cover a 2- x 3-foot (60-cm x 90-cm) surface. Butter the top of the dough and mound the filling (apples, pears, mushrooms, fish, chicken, etc.) across the smallest end. (By pulling up one end of the tablecloth, the strudel will roll into a cylinder shape.) Twist off your strudel like sausage links to fit onto your baking sheet. Brush the tops with melted butter and bake for 15 minutes.

Ravioli Dough

Perfect ravioli dough is soft, tender, and pliable. After working just once with this dough and making ravioli pockets, it will become your favorite pasta course. This recipe gives you a lot of choice: you can make a few small ravioli or one jumbo-sized one. You can also vary the stuffing mixture. You can make extra ravioli, space them out on a tray and freeze them for later use; they'll be just as good as when you make them fresh. A small pasta roller machine makes this recipe easier, but the same results can be achieved with a rolling pin—it just takes a little longer!

1/3 cup	milk	80 mL
1/3 cup	vegetable oil	80 mL
6	large eggs	6
3 1/2 cups	flour	840 mL

Combine the milk, oil, and eggs in a mixer with the dough hook attachment. Slowly pour in the flour until a soft, completely mixed dough ball is formed. Wrap the dough in plastic wrap and chill for 30 minutes. Will keep well in the refrigerator for 2 days.

Follow the directions for your pasta machine to roll out the dough gradually from thick to thin. If using a rolling pin, it will take a while to work the dough down to about 1/16-inch (2 mm) in thickness.

Cocktailing

Although the word "cocktailing" cannot be found in a dictionary, it's a word that should suggest a real feeling of fun. A good reception or cocktail party can last for hours and, with the right food, can replace a dinner party, allowing you to have people meet more casually—to drink, snack, and mingle all at the same time. Finger foods serve the purpose of settling your guests' hunger, as well as balancing the consumption of alcohol with food so that the party does not end too early for some of the guests. The finger foods should be consumable in one to two bites and should consist of just a few flavors and textures. The recipes in this section have been geared for a smaller gathering of about four people, but can easily be multiplied by two or three for larger gatherings or when it is the only food being served.

It is imperative to have food fun at free-spirited gatherings like these, so I recommend that you have fun with presentations and taste combinations. Create a theme for your reception with the types of foods and serving dishes that you use—get creative with your china and glassware. If you are having a formal dinner party, serving one or two of these dishes as hors d'oeuvres helps make a great first impression and hints of the good food to come. The following pages will show you some new ways of reception entertaining. Cocktailing—a great way to party.

Seafood Tempura Skewers

Serves 4

A great party food—crispy textures with the great tastes of basil and seafood. This recipe features shrimp and scallops in Tempura Batter, page 31. Serve with a beautiful Lemon Cream Dip, page 31. Party on!

4	jumbo shrimp, fresh or frozen	4
4	scallops, fresh or frozen	4
1	bulb fennel	1
1	large red pepper	1
1 recipe	Tempura Batter (page 31)	1 recipe
8	large fresh basil leaves	8
	oil for deep-frying	
	salt to taste	

Place eight 6-inch (15-cm) wooden skewers in water for at least 30 minutes to prevent burning later. Meanwhile, peel and devein the shrimp, then cut in half lengthwise. Cut the scallops in half. Cut the fennel and red pepper into 1-inch (2.5-cm) squares. Assemble the skewers, using only the front half of the skewer (farthest from the end you use to hold it), in the following order: ½ scallop, basil leaf, fennel, ½ shrimp, basil leaf, and red pepper. Repeat on all 8 skewers.

Preheat oil in a deep fryer to 350˚ F (175˚C). Dip the prepared skewers, one by one, in the tempura batter and deep-fry for 3–5 minutes for a medium–well-done finish. To remove any excess oil, pat the skewers with a paper towel. Season immediately with salt.

For an effective presentation, push the finished skewers into a fresh pineapple, a Chinese eggplant, a daikon radish, or just let your imagination take over.

 Olaf's Tip: Keep the vegetables thinly sliced and all ingredients consistently shaped for even cooking.

Potato Skins for Grown-Ups

Serves 4

Potato skins are a great "vessel" for delicious toppings. I took this rustic appetizer and finished it with a ritzy topping of smoked salmon. A great combo—both crispy and soft! Ordinary potato skins will never taste the same again.

2	large Yukon Gold or russet potatoes	2
	vegetable oil for frying	
	salt and pepper to taste	
8	slices smoked salmon	8
1 recipe	Lemon Cream Dip (page 31)	1 recipe
2 Tbsp.	caviar	30 mL
	fresh dill for garnish	

Wash and scrub clean the potatoes. Bake until tender. Cut into quarters and remove the flesh part of the potato from each wedge, leaving about 1/8-inch (.3 cm) of potato on the skin.

With the oil at 350° F (175°C), deep-fry the potato skins until crispy and pat off any excess oil. Season with salt and pepper. At serving time, warm up the skins in a 350° F (175°C) oven for about 5 minutes.

To assemble, top each potato skin wedge with half a slice of smoked salmon, some Lemon Cream Dip, a bit of caviar, and a small sprig of dill to top it off.

 Olaf's Tip: For crispy potato skins, make sure you don't leave too much potato on them. To make use of the potato flesh, freeze it and use in my Cream of Roast Garlic Soup, page 70. An alternate for caviar could be capers or chopped chives.

Makes 2 cups (480 mL)

Peppery arugula leaves and Asiago cheese are a great marriage of flavor. This also makes a fantastic butter substitute for spreading on breads.

¼ cup	pecans	60 mL
2 cups	arugula	480 mL
½ cup	fresh basil leaves	120 mL
1	clove garlic	1
½ cup	grated Asiago cheese	120 mL
1 tsp.	sea salt	5 mL
¼ tsp.	black pepper	1.2 mL
1 cup	olive oil	240 mL
20	won ton wrappers	20
	salt and white pepper to taste	

Place pecans on a baking sheet and bake in oven for 5 minutes at 350° F (150°C) until the nuts are lightly golden in color.

In a food processor, place arugula, basil, garlic, pecans, cheese, salt, and pepper. With the food processor running, slowly add in the olive oil. Will keep in the refrigerator for 7 days.

Preheat the oil in a deep fryer to 350° F (175°C) and quickly deep-fry the won ton wrappers, a few at a time, for about 60 seconds. Pat off the excess oil with a paper towel and immediately season with salt and pepper.

I know you will serve this dip often, so to vary your presentation, try it with vegetable crudités, toasted pita, or Mediterranean breads.

 Olaf's Tip: Make sure the garlic is fresh and is in the food processor when blending the green leaves to ensure the leaves retain their brilliant green color. It's the essential oils found in the garlic that, when introduced to the chlorophyl of the green leaves, work together to maintain that color.

Charred Vegetable Tapenade

Makes 8 cups (2 L)

A very versatile dish. I recommend using it as a spread or dip with a toasted French stick, grilled Portuguese cornbread, and/or mini-pitas. It can also be used as a condiment or topping with main entrées such as grilled fish or meats!

1	red pepper, quartered	1
1	yellow pepper, quartered	1
1	red onion, sliced	1
1	small eggplant, quartered	1
1	small zucchini, quartered	1
2	hot chili peppers, chopped	2
2	cloves garlic, minced	2
1 cup	chopped fresh parsley	240 mL
2	tomatoes, diced	2
½ cup	diced black olives	120 mL
1 cup	olive oil	240 mL
	salt and pepper to taste	
½ cup	ketchup	120 mL
½ cup	finely chopped fresh basil leaves	120 mL

On a medium-hot barbecue or on a baking sheet under the oven broiler, grill the quartered peppers, onion, eggplant, and zucchini until very well-charred. When cool enough to handle, chop into ⅛-inch (.3-cm) pieces. Place in a food processor and add the chili peppers, garlic, parsley, tomatoes, and olives. With the food processor still running, pulse until creamy, then slowly drizzle in the olive oil. Taste and add the seasonings. Fold in the ketchup and basil. Will keep in the refrigerator for 3–4 days. If using bread, slice and toast the bread in the oven, then spoon a dollop of tapenade on each slice.

I suggest you present this vegetarian delight on a wooden paddle board or even a checker game board. Line up the grilled bread rounds and top with this tapenade.

 Olaf's Tip: Ketchup!!! Yes—the sweetness helps to balance the acidity and bitterness of the tomato–eggplant combination.

Roasted Red Pepper and Tomato Dip

Makes 6 cups (1.5 L)

Roasted red peppers and vine-ripened tomatoes—two great ingredients and unique flavors pulsed together. Great as a dip or topping, and it can also be used as a relish to jazz up sandwiches, burgers, and anything else that needs some boost!

3	red peppers, quartered	3
1	small red onion, diced	1
3	ripe tomatoes, diced	3
1	scallion, finely sliced	1
1	lime, juice of	1
1 Tbsp.	sugar	15 mL
1 cup	ketchup	240 mL
1	clove garlic, minced	1
½ cup	olive oil	120 mL
½ cup	chopped fresh parsley	120 mL
¼ cup	chopped fresh basil	60 mL
	salt to taste	
1 tsp.	fresh cracked black peppercorns	5 mL

If you have a gas burner or barbecue grill, use it to roast the quartered peppers; otherwise, place the peppers on a baking sheet under your oven broiler. When completely charred and blistered, immediately place in a bowl, cover with plastic wrap, and let sit for 5 minutes. Carefully peel off the skin and dice.

In a bowl, mix all the ingredients together. This dip will keep in the refrigerator for a 3–5 days. Serve with Italian herb focaccia bread points, grilled pita, French stick, olive bread, or Crispy Flatbread, page 34.

For presentation, try to find Mexican-style serving pieces such as clay or earthenware dishes, handwoven baskets, or clay tiles from a local hardware store.

 Olaf's Tip: When roasting peppers, don't peel the skin under running water or you will wash away the flavor. After peeling the charred skin and removing the seeds, place the peppers in a bowl before dicing to catch the great liquid that will make this dip a step up!

Black Bean and Roasted Banana Dip

Serves 4

Yes it sounds really odd, but roasted bananas, black beans, and spices from the American Southwest make an unusual combination that must be tried at your next gathering. It's a twist on a Tex Mex cuisine. Serve with corn chips for a fun, casual dip.

2 cups	dry black beans	480 mL
2 cups	vegetable oil	480 mL
1	large onion, sliced	1
2	bananas, sliced	2
2	cloves garlic, minced	2
1 Tbsp.	hot pepper sauce	15 mL
1½ Tbsp.	chili powder	22.5 mL
1½ Tbsp.	cumin	22.5 mL
¼ cup	tomato paste	60 mL
½ cup	ketchup	120 mL
1	jalapeño pepper, finely diced	1
2	limes, juice of	2
	salt and white pepper to taste	

In a large pot, place 10 cups (2.4 L) of unsalted water and the black beans. Simmer for 30–45 minutes until tender. In a medium pan, place 1 cup (240 mL) of the oil. Roast the onion and bananas until golden brown. Add the garlic, hot pepper sauce, and spices and sauté for 2 minutes. Add the tomato paste and cook for an additional 4 minutes.

Set aside ½ cup (120 mL) of the steamed black beans and add the rest to the onion and banana mix. Place the mixture into a food processor and purée. Add the ketchup, jalapeño pepper, lime juice, and drizzle in the remaining oil. Add the seasonings to taste. Fold in the remaining ½ cup (120 mL) of beans for added texture. Serve warm or at room temperature with crispy corn chips. Will keep in the refrigerator for 2 days.

Olaf's Tip: Don't add salt to the water when cooking any type of bean or any legume as this makes the outer skin stay tough, never tender. Canned drained black beans can be used, but add them directly into the roasted onion and banana mixture.

Quark and Garden Herbs Dip

Makes 4½ cups (1 L)

There are many types of dips, but this one features real garden freshness with the lightness of a yogurt base to make a really tasty dip. To present it, hollow out mini-pumpernickel buns and fill with the dip for individual servings, or place the dip in a decorative bowl and serve with bite-sized cubes of larger pumpernickel bread.

2 cups	quark* or cream cheese	480 mL
1 cup	yogurt	240 mL
½ cup	sour cream	120 mL
1	lemon, juice of	1
1 tsp.	salt	5 mL
	cayenne pepper to taste	
½ cup	chopped fresh dill	120 mL
1	bundle fresh chives, finely sliced	1
1 cup	fresh parsley, finely chopped	240 mL
2	stalks celery, finely diced	2
1 cup	peeled, finely grated cucumber	240 mL
½ cup	finely grated carrot	120 mL
	*See Glossary, page 203.	

Mix together the quark, yogurt, sour cream, lemon juice, salt, and cayenne pepper. Fold in the herbs and vegetables. Chill.

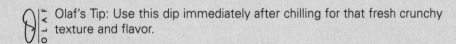 Olaf's Tip: Use this dip immediately after chilling for that fresh crunchy texture and flavor.

Smoked Bacon, Onion,
Sour Cream, and Herb Tart

Serves 4 (or 32 pieces)

This is a great snack for a wine tasting! It's a perfect fit with a glass of Gewürztraminer; the many strong flavors make this wine dance. This is a great item to make up the day before and bake just before serving.

1 lb.	puff pastry, store-purchased, thawed	455 g
⅓ cup	sour cream	80 mL
1	clove garlic, minced	1
½ lb.	double-smoked bacon*, diced, rind removed	225 g
1	small Spanish onion, finely chopped	1
1	leek, white only, super-finely sliced	1
1 Tbsp.	fresh chopped thyme	15 mL
¼ cup	fresh chopped parsley	60 mL
	salt and pepper to taste	

*See Glossary, page 202.

Preheat the oven to 350°F (175°C). Roll out the puff pastry into a square approximately 12- x 12-inches (30-cm x 30-cm) and ⅛-inch (.3 cm) in thickness. Using a fork, prick the dough all over. Combine the sour cream and the minced garlic and thinly spread the mixture over the dough. Place the remaining ingredients evenly, one by one, over the sour cream mixture. Don't go over the side and waste any of the delicious flavors.

Slow bake for approximately 30–35 minutes, or until the crust is a golden brown. Let cool 2–3 minutes before cutting into bite-sized pieces. Try cutting into 3-inch (7.5-cm) squares and then cut again on the diagonal for nice-sized triangular pieces. Serve warm.

 Olaf's Tip: After rolling out the dough, let it rest for 10 minutes to prevent it from being tough.

Italian Croissant Surprise

Serves 4

Wakey wakey! It's an Italian breakfast! But it's not just for breakfast anymore. This croissant, with its soft milky cheese, salty Parma ham, sweet basil, and finely cracked pepper is perfect for a party at any time of day.

4	pieces bocconcini cheese, halved	4
1 Tbsp.	cracked black peppercorns	15 mL
8	fresh basil leaves, whole	8
8	slices prosciutto ham	8
1 lb.	puff pastry, store-purchased, thawed	455 g
1	large egg, beaten	1
¼ cup	water	60 mL

Preheat the oven to 350°F (175°C). Roll the cheese pieces in the cracked peppercorns to coat. Wrap with basil leaves and ham. Roll the puff pastry out to ⅛-inch (.3-cm) thick. Cut into eight triangles 5 inches (12.5 cm) wide and about 3 inches (7.5 cm) in height. Make a wash with the beaten egg and water and lightly brush the wide end of the triangle. This will seal the pastry when you roll it. Now place the cheese rolls at the wide end of the triangle and roll up like a croissant. Brush the entire outside surface with the remaining egg wash. Bake for approximately 15 minutes or until puffed and light golden brown.

 Olaf's Tip: Don't use too much bocconcini cheese because it does melt like water—although I like to have a little run out so it makes crispy corners, which look very rustic. If you are really pressed for time, ready-to-bake croissants could be used instead of the puff pastry.

B-52 Tomato Shooters with Raw Oysters

Makes eight 3-oz. (85-g) shooters

When we competed in Dallas, Texas, at the World Banqueting Competition at the Fairmount Hotel, we were given a lot of oysters! This recipe is one that Team Canada prepared for the "Reception Hors d'oeuvres" category. Shot-gun the oyster and knock back the shooter. And watch out for the vodka!

Part 1: The Shooters

½ cup	finely diced carrot	120 mL
½ cup	finely diced red pepper	120 mL
½ cup	finely diced English cucumber	120 mL
½ cup	finely diced red onion	120 mL
⅓ cup	chopped fresh chives	80 mL
2 cups	roughly chopped ripe red tomatoes	480 mL
½	clove garlic, minced	½
1 Tbsp.	olive oil	15 mL
1 Tbsp.	red wine vinegar	15 mL
dash	hot pepper sauce	dash
	salt and white pepper to taste	
2 cups	roughly chopped ripe yellow tomatoes	480 mL
1	lemon, juice of	1
4 oz.	vodka	113 mL
2	green onions for garnish	2
8	Malpeque oysters, freshly shucked	8
1	lemon, quartered	1
⅓ cup	celery salt (to rim glasses)	80 mL

Toss the carrot, red pepper, cucumber, red onion, and chives together and divide equally into 3 bowls.

Layer 3 – In a food processor, purée the red tomatoes and garlic. Add the olive oil, vinegar, and hot pepper sauce until mixed. Strain into a bowl. Mix this vegetable juice with the third of the diced vegetables (in one of the 3 bowls) and add salt and pepper to taste. Chill.

Layer 2 – In a food processor, purée the yellow tomatoes. Strain. Mix with the next third of the diced vegetables and season to taste. Chill.

Layer 1 – Mix the lemon juice and vodka with the last third of the diced vegetables.

Part 2: Preparing the Garnish

Use approximately 6 inches (15 cm) of the green of the onion only. With a paring knife, cut the greens finely lengthwise and place the slices in a bowl of ice water. Watch the onion ends curl.

Part 3: The Assembly

Place one shucked oyster on each of 8 side plates.

Dip the rim of the shooter glasses in the lemon juice, then roll in celery salt and place a glass on each plate.

Fill the shooter glasses in 3 layers.

Layer 1 – lemon–vodka mix

Layer 2 – yellow tomato purée

Layer 3 – spicy red tomato purée

Garnish with the green onion curls.

Olaf's Tip: The 3 layers can be made up to a day ahead and kept chilled until you're ready to go. Don't pour the different mixtures directly into the shooter glass. Pour them carefully over a spoon to keep the colorful layers separate.

Escargot in a Pastry Pillow

Serves 4

My family's favorite! I always have to make this appetizer for family potluck parties. The Tarragon Cream Sauce blends beautifully with the garlic and escargot whether served in a bowl to dunk the pastry pillows into or when pooled on a plate with the pillows on top. Although escargot scares some people off, this dish will win over any newcomer to the flavor. The first impression is lasting!

Part 1: Tarragon Cream Sauce
Makes 1½ cups (360 mL)

2 Tbsp.	unsalted butter	30 mL
3	shallots, finely diced	3
1	clove garlic, minced	1
¼ cup	red wine vinegar	60 mL
1½ cups	35% cream	360 mL
2 Tbsp.	fresh chopped tarragon (save the stems)	30 mL
	salt and pepper to taste	
1	cayenne pepper to taste	1
1	sprig fresh thyme for garnish	1

In a medium pot over medium-low heat, sweat the shallots, garlic, and tarragon stems in butter until soft. Pour in the red wine vinegar and simmer until the vinegar has completely evaporated. Stir in the cream and tarragon leaves, then strain through a fine mesh strainer. Season with salt, pepper, and cayenne to taste. This sauce can be made 1–2 days ahead, chilled, and reheated in the microwave.

 Olaf's Tip: For maximum flavor, use all the tarragon stems and not-so-perfect leaves in the vinegar reduction.

Part 2: The Pillows

2	shallots, finely diced	2
2	cloves garlic, minced	2
¼ cup	butter	60 mL
16	large canned escargots, drained	16
1 cup	dry white wine	240 mL
	salt and pepper to taste	
¼ cup	chopped fresh parsley	60 mL
1 lb.	puff pastry, store-purchased, thawed	455 g
½ cup	herb cream cheese, store-purchased	120 mL
1	large egg, beaten	1
1 Tbsp.	water	15 mL

In a pan, sweat the shallots and garlic in butter over a medium-low heat until softened. Add escargots and sauté until warmed. Stir in the white wine. Continue to sauté until the wine is reduced to a glaze. Taste and season with salt and pepper. Remove from heat and stir in the parsley.

Preheat the oven to 350°F (175°C). Roll out the puff pastry to ⅛-inch (.3-cm) thick. Cut into ten 2-x 2-inch (5-cm x 5-cm) squares. Combine the beaten egg and water and lightly wash the perimeter of the squares. Lay a teaspoon-sized (5-mL) piece of cheese mixture into the center, and add 1 escargot. Bring up the sides and corners to make a small bag or pillow and squeeze to seal. Lightly brush the entire outside surface with the egg wash. Bake for approximately 20 minutes or until puffed and light golden brown. For easy entertaining, prepare the day before and bake just before serving.

Presentation: Puddle a quarter of the sauce in the center of a warmed plate and gently float a pastry pillow on it. Garnish with a sprig of fresh tarragon.

Olaf's Tip: Once the pillow is made, let the pastry rest for approximately 20 minutes before baking so you can get the maximum lift of the puff pastry.

Smoked Chicken and Leek
Poppers with Herb Mayonnaise

Makes 30 1-oz. (28-g) pieces

For an eye-catching presentation, place a patty on a tablespoon or soup spoon and drop a dollop of Herb Mayonnaise (page 30) on the patty. Place the spoons around a serving tray and watch your guests' faces when they see these amazing treats. Your guests can say they've been "spoon-fed."

⅓ cup	unsalted butter	80 mL
2 cups	finely sliced smoked chicken or turkey	480 mL
1	leek, white only, sliced	1
½ cup	finely sliced green onions	120 mL
1 cup	diced onions	240 mL
¼ cup	chopped fresh parsley	60 mL
2	large egg yolks	2
20	crackers (your favorite), crushed	20
	salt and pepper to taste	
1 recipe	Herb Mayonnaise (page 30)	1 recipe

Preheat the oven to 350°F (175°C). In a frying pan, sauté in butter the chicken, leek, and onions. There should be no color; just wilt the vegetables. Place in a bowl and add the egg yolks, crackers, salt, and pepper. Mix until the mixture is dry but sticky to the touch. Now form walnut-sized patties that will fit onto a soup spoon. Place patties onto a baking tray lined with parchment. Bake for 5–8 minutes. These patties can be made ahead and frozen. Thaw before baking.

 Olaf's Tip: If too sticky to roll in your hands, add more crackers or bread crumbs.

Mango and Lobster–Stuffed Cherry Tomatoes

Makes 20 pieces

Putting on the ritz! A simple, elegant, expensive-looking hors d'oeuvre. Cherry tomatoes are the perfect bite-sized vessel for this wonderful seafood salad.

6 oz.	lobster meat or tiger shrimp, cooked	170 g
1	mango, finely diced	1
1	roasted red pepper, finely diced	1
1 Tbsp.	sliced fresh tarragon	15 mL
½ cup	cream cheese, room temperature	120 mL
1 oz.	brandy	28 g
	salt and pepper to taste	
2 cups	cherry tomatoes	480 mL
	dill sprigs for garnish	

Finely dice the lobster meat or tiger shrimp, then press out the liquid through a sieve or squeeze out by hand. Add the mango, red pepper, tarragon, cream cheese, and brandy. Add the seasonings. With a very sharp knife, carefully remove a slice from the top of each tomato. Hollow out the tomatoes with a demitasse spoon or small melon baller and stuff with the seafood mixture.

The filling can be made the day before, but fill the tomatoes the day you're going to serve them. To change the presentation you could place the tomatoes in small truffle wrappers similar to muffin liners (available at party or baking supply stores) and arrange on a platter. Top each tomato with a sprig of dill.

 Olaf's Tip: The cherry tomatoes should be ripe but not to the point of being soft, making them difficult to handle. With a very sharp knife, take a small slice off the bottom of each tomato to ensure that it sits flat.

Savory Cheese Truffles

Makes about 12 truffles

Here are two great variations of a cheese appetizer that will impress any guest. The process is the same, but the flavors are wildly different!

Red Pepper, Brie, and Pumpernickel Truffles

1 cup	Brie, room temperature	240 mL
½ cup	cream cheese, room temperature	120 mL
1	red pepper, roasted (see page 43)	1
¼ cup	finely chopped fresh parsley	60 mL
	salt and white pepper to taste	
1 cup	fresh pumpernickel crumbs	240 mL

Goat Cheese and Pistachio Truffles

1 cup	pistachios, shelled	240 mL
1½ cups	goat cheese	360 mL
¼ cup	fresh, finely sliced chives	60 mL
1 tsp.	minced garlic	5 mL
½ tsp.	paprika	2.5 mL
	salt and pepper to taste	

In a food processor, blend the Brie, cream cheese, red pepper, parsley, salt, and pepper. Make 1-inch (2.5-cm) balls, then roll them in the pumpernickel crumbs.

Preheat the oven to 300°F (150°C) and place the pistachios on a baking sheet. Bake for 5 minutes or until light brown in color and then finely chop.

In a food processor, blend the goat cheese, chives, garlic, and paprika. Add seasonings. Again, form into balls, and roll them in the finely chopped pistachios.

Once the cheese truffles are all rolled, arrange them in a color pattern on the serving plate. These can be made a day ahead and stored in a covered container in the refrigerator until ready to serve.

 Olaf's Tip: Toasting the pistachio nuts allows the oils to be expressed and results in maximum flavor.

Starters and Palate-Teasers

The starter of a menu is the way to get the culinary expedition rolling. One way to start off the menu is with something acidic, such as a vinaigrette or another very strong jolt of flavor, such as a small portion of a special soup. First impressions are lasting and, with a strong introduction, your menu is well underway.

Acidity is important in waking up the stomach and preparing it for the food courses that are to come. In my salads, therefore, you will find a lot of strong vinegar flavors. I am not a particularly big fan of a lettuce-only salad; I guess that would be just too easy.

My soups are also very rich in flavor and therefore also make a strong start to the dining experience. I prefer hearty soups, like chowders—soups that have been nurtured for hours. But they can't be too "pasty-thick" in texture.

On a lighter side, I enjoy serving mousses that are so light, I call them "foams"! These light servings really pack a punch of flavor.

I am very passionate about the appetizer kitchen, and early in my culinary education, I fell in love with this style of cooking. Here you have a little more time to build your plates because there are few temperature restraints or hot-and-cold combination plates. You have time to build your cold salad showpiece.

Your first courses have arrived. Everyone take your seats. A culinary experience is about to begin.

Salad from the Market

Serves 4

I love to build compound salads—and "build" is the key word. By stacking the vegetables in layers on the plate you can really make an impression with the individual flavors. Like the other salad dressings I use, this two-minute blender dressing makes a fantastic topping. I picture this salad with seasonal vegetables and lettuces that have just been picked up at the market, with fresh, crisp textures. I have suggested a market combination here, but feel free to use what you like and can find fresh.

Part 1: Light of Heart Dressing

Makes 1½ cups (360 mL)

1 cup	water	240 mL
¼ cup	olive oil	60 mL
⅛ cup	tarragon vinegar	30 mL
½ tsp.	Dijon mustard	2.5 mL
2 Tbsp.	sugar	30 mL
⅛ cup	white wine vinegar	30 mL
½ cup	vegetable oil	120 mL
½	lemon, juice of	½
	salt and white pepper to taste	

Place all the ingredients into a blender or food processor and mix well. This can be kept in the refrigerator for up to 7 days. Reblend or whisk before each use.

Part 2: Market Finds

½ cup	green beans, blanched tender	120 mL
2	vine-ripened tomatoes, quartered	2
½ lb.	green asparagus tips, blanched tender	225 g
1 cup	finely sliced cucumber	240 mL
1 cup	finely diced carrot	240 mL
5 oz.	mixed lettuces	140 g

To assemble, on four plates, make a base with the beans. Then layer the tomatoes, then the asparagus, then the cucumbers, and carrots stacked on top. Drizzle some of the dressing over this. Toss the mixed lettuces with the rest of the dressing and build as a top on this tower of veggies.

Olaf's Tip: The water makes this dressing so light that there is no oil taste, making it an especially light and flavorful topping.

Cashew-Crusted Scallops
with Asian Vegetable Salad

Serves 4

I've made several versions of this salad over the years for my wife. This combination of roasted scallops, crunchy cashews, balsamic vinegar, and crispy Asian vegetables is absolutely fantastic! If you're at all intimidated by this more complex recipe, try my simplified version, explained in "Olaf's Tip." But for the more adventurous chef, try this recipe as written for a beautiful taste and appearance.

Part 1: Scallops

12	jumbo scallops	12
	salt and cracked black peppercorns to taste	
1/3 cup	flour	80 mL
1/2 cup	olive oil	120 mL
1/4 cup	unsalted butter, room temperature	60 mL

Season the scallops with salt and pepper, dust with flour to give them a crispier texture, and pat off any excess. Heat the oil in a very hot pan and sear the scallops quickly—a minute on both sides. Add the butter and cook until brown. Remove from the pan, and pat off any excess oil.

Part 2: Cashew Crust

2 cups	salted cashews	480 mL
2 Tbsp.	unsalted butter	30 mL
12	fresh basil leaves, chopped	12
1 tsp.	paprika	5 mL
1 tsp.	minced garlic	5 mL
	salt and black pepper to taste	
1/2 cup	grainy mustard	120 mL

Toast 24 cashews in a 350°F (175°C) oven for 4 minutes, then set aside. Reduce the oven to 300°F (150°C). Place the rest of the cashews in a food processor with the rest of the ingredients and pulse to a crumbly consistency.

Place the seared scallops on a baking sheet and top each with ¼ tsp. (1.2 mL) of grainy mustard. Spread evenly. Pack on ½-inch (1.2 cm) of the Cashew Crust. Bake for 4 minutes, or until golden brown.

Part 3: Asian Vegetable Salad

Serves 4

½ cup	julienned daikon radish	120 mL
½ cup	bean sprouts	120 mL
2	green onions, finely sliced	2
1	small red onion, finely diced	1
⅓ cup	pea sprouts	80 mL
½	red pepper, julienned	½
½	yellow pepper, julienned	½
½ lb.	asparagus, blanched tender, ¼-inch (.6-cm) diagonal slices	225 g
1 Tbsp.	chopped fresh coriander leaves	15 mL
1	small carrot, julienned	1
	salt and pepper to taste	

Prepare the salad by mixing all the ingredients and tossing with Honey Balsamic Vinaigrette, page 18. Place the warm crusted scallops on top of the salad and garnish with toasted cashews.

Olaf's Tip: Any combination of any of these vegetables would be workable. During the preparation, slice the vegetables and store separately in containers with ice cold water and refrigerate.

For the simplified version of this recipe, roast scallops in olive oil in a good frying pan. Add cashews and other vegetables to the same frying pan. Drizzle balsamic vinegar into the scallops and cashew mixture. Toss in a bowl with mixed lettuce greens.

Wacky, Tacky Shrimp Cocktail

Serves 4

This is the way to start off a seriously fun dinner party: cocktail glasses brimming with delicate shrimp and a funky combination of vegetable and fruit, with a light dressing to pull it all together. Big wow factor!

Part 1: The Shrimp

20	jumbo tiger shrimp, peeled and deveined	20
1 recipe	Court Bouillon (page 24)	1 recipe

Poach the shrimp for 3 minutes in the boiling court bouillon. Spoon out the shrimps to stop them cooking, and chill the bouillon. When the bouillon is completely chilled, return the shrimp to it to keep them moist. This part can be done a day ahead and the bouillon and shrimp kept in the refrigerator.

Part 2: The Cocktail

2	pink grapefruits, in segments	2
1	avocado, diced	1
2	sprigs fresh dill, chopped	2
1	English cucumber, peeled and diced	1

Toss together.

Part 3: Spritzer Dressing

1	lime, juice of	1
1	lemon, juice of	1
	salt and pepper to taste	
½ cup	grapeseed oil or canola oil	120 mL
1 cup	mineral water	240 mL
1 cup	champagne or sparkling wine	240 mL

Combine the first 5 ingredients and set aside. Just before serving, add the champagne or sparkling wine.

Part 4: The Assembly

wooden skewers

tropical fruits (kiwi, pineapple) and strawberries

cocktail umbrellas

margarita or martini glasses

To assemble, toss the shrimps and the cocktail ingredients in the dressing and fill up the glasses with this mixture. Thread the fruits onto a skewer and place it in the glass, then top it off with an umbrella.

Olaf's Tip: If you want to make this ahead of time, assemble the glasses and set in the refrigerator. At the last minute, add the mineral water and champagne or sparkling wine.

Duet of Asparagus

Serves 4

To many people, especially Europeans, fresh white and green asparagus signals the first sign of spring. This dish is light eating—great for a patio luncheon. I suggest you check with the produce manager at your grocery store for availability of white asparagus. This is a relatively simple-to-make dish that will really knock the socks off your guests.

Part 1: The Asparagus

1 lb.	white asparagus	455 g
1 lb.	green asparagus	455 g
¼ cup	sugar	60 mL
⅛ cup	salt	30 mL
3	oranges, juice of	3
1	lemon, juice of	1

Using a vegetable peeler, peel all the asparagus by removing the sides of the stalks an inch from the tips. In 4¼ cups (1 L) of boiling salted water, blanch the green asparagus till tender, drain well, and place in an ice bath to stop the cooking process.

For the white asparagus, in a new pot, boil another 4¼ cups (1 L) water and add the sugar, salt, and the juices of the orange and lemon. Place the white asparagus in the "brine" and cook until tender. Drain well and immediately place in ice water. Keep the "brine" for the dressing.

Part 2: The Dressing

2 cups	white asparagus brine	480 mL
1 cup	white wine vinegar	240 mL
1 cup	vegetable oil	240 mL
1 tsp.	Dijon mustard	5 mL
1 Tbsp.	sugar	15 mL
	salt and white pepper to taste	
1 cup	mixed lettuces	240 mL
2	medium tomatoes, seeded, diced	2
2	oranges, peeled, in segments	2
6	sprigs fresh chives, finely chopped	6

In a blender or food processor, place 2 cups (480 mL) of the brine and combine with three stalks of the cooked white asparagus, vinegar, vegetable oil, mustard, sugar, salt, and pepper. Blend for 2 minutes. Taste and adjust the seasonings. Strain through a fine sieve to remove any unblended pieces.

Presentation: To present this dish, use an oversized plate and fan out the white and green asparagus. Cover the bottoms of the spears with the mixed lettuces. Spread the tomato, oranges, and chives randomly. Use lots of dressing for the asparagus to soak up.

Olaf's Tip: The citrus and the sweetness of the white asparagus brine offsets the bitterness of this type of asparagus.

Towering Smoked Salmon to the Stars with Grainy Mustard Sambuca Sauce

Serves 4

A shooting-star starter, a classic made new. Smoked salmon and mustard sauce is a classic combo, but by adding brown sugar, honey, and sambuca to the sauce you take this dish to another level. Capers, onions, and dill are another classic combo, but add the crispy buttery pastry layers and you have another twist in texture and body. This is pictured on the cover.

Part 1: Grainy Mustard Sambuca Sauce
Makes 3 cups (720 mL)

2	large egg yolks	2
2 Tbsp.	brown sugar	30 mL
¼ cup	honey	60 mL
1 Tbsp.	white vinegar	15 mL
1	lemon, juice of	1
½ cup	grainy mustard	120 mL
	salt and white pepper to taste	
¼ cup	white sambuca	60 mL
1 cup	vegetable oil	240 mL

Mix all the ingredients except the oil together in a blender or food processor and while the machine is still running, slowly pour the oil into the mixture until emulsified. Check seasonings.

Olaf's Tip: This is a great honey mustard sauce for use with fish, chicken, or pork. The sambuca is optional, but makes it fun for big kids!

Part 2: The Towers

2 lbs.	puff pastry, store-purchased, thawed	900 g
1	large egg	1
¼ cup	whole milk	60 mL
2 cups	cream cheese, room temperature	480 mL
½ cup	chopped fresh chives	120 mL
1 cup	chopped fresh spinach	240 mL
	salt and white pepper to taste	
16	slices smoked salmon	16
1	medium red onion, finely cut rings	1
¼ cup	small capers	60 mL
1	small tomato, peeled and diced	1
1	sprig fresh dill, chopped	1
1	sprig fresh chervil, chopped	1

Preheat the oven to 350°F (175°C). Roll out the puff pastry to ¼-inch (.6-cm) thickness and with a star cookie cutter, cut out 12 stars. Combine the egg and milk to make a wash and brush on just the *top* of the pastry. Bake 10 minutes until golden brown. Cool and cut horizontally in half.

Blend the cream cheese, chives, spinach, salt, and white pepper.

OLAF Olaf's Tip: When egg washing the stars, do not let any egg wash run over the sides of the pastry or it will not rise.

Presentation: Spoon about ⅛ cup (30 mL) of the Grainy Mustard Sambuca Sauce into the center of your serving plates. Start building towers: star pastry, spinach cream cheese, smoked salmon, onions, capers, and then repeat those layers. End with the third star pastry and garnish by sprinkling capers, the diced tomato, dill, and chervil around the tower.

Red Lentil Soup
with Breaded Sausage Croutons

Serves 4

A typical rustic German soup taken to a white tablecloth presentation. This hearty combination of vegetables and legumes might be unfamiliar to some, but is really an interesting blend of flavors. Trust me, people will love this soup!

Part 1: The Soup

2 cups	dry red lentils	480 mL
1	carrot, finely diced	1
1	celery stalk, finely diced	1
½ cup	unsalted butter	120 mL
¼ lb.	double-smoked bacon*, rind removed	113 g
2	small onions, finely diced	2
1	clove garlic, minced	1
½ cup	tomato paste	120 mL
2	sprigs fresh thyme, chopped	2
6 cups	Chicken Stock (page 21)	1.5 L
1	bay leaf	1
	salt and white pepper to taste	
	*See Glossary, page 202.	

Before preparing this soup, it is advisable to soak the lentils in cold water for about 3 hours.

For the garnish, set aside half the diced carrot and celery. In a medium pot, melt the butter and sweat off the bacon, onion, garlic, and remaining carrot and celery. Add the tomato paste, lentils, and thyme and simmer for 3 minutes. Then add the chicken stock and bay leaf. Simmer about 30 minutes and then purée. Taste and adjust the seasonings. Bring to a boil and then simmer until thickened. Watch very carefully and keep stirring so as not to burn on the bottom.

Part 2: Breaded Sausage Croutons

½ cup	finely chopped fresh parsley	120 mL
¼ cup	finely chopped fresh chives	60 mL
4 cups	fresh white bread crumbs*	960 mL
2	large bratwurst	2
2	large eggs	2
¼ cup	milk	60 mL
½ cup	vegetable oil for frying	120 mL
1 Tbsp.	unsalted butter	15 mL
	salt and pepper to taste	
	*See Glossary, page 202.	

Toss together the parsley, chives, and bread crumbs. On low heat, simmer the sausages for about 8–10 minutes, or until fully cooked, then slice into ¼-inch (.6-cm) slices. Combine the egg and milk to make a wash and, using your hands, firmly press the sausage pieces first into the wash and then into the crumb mixture. On medium heat, combine the oil and butter and fry the coated sausage rounds until golden brown. Drain on a paper towel and season immediately. Can be refrigerated for 3–5 days or frozen for 2–3 months

Presentation: Float the diced carrots and celery and the crispy breaded sausages, acting as croutons, into the soup just before serving.

Gar-"Licky" Escargot and Barley Chowder

Serves 4

Tastes so good you'll "lick" your bowl clean. Let's cross the line of everyday cuisine. Picture the escargots with a supporting cast of flavors: smokey, garlicky, with thick cream and tarragon. This soup originated in the Black Forest region of Germany where the best escargots were found in the wine hills of the area. This is an unforgettable soup, even if your hunt for escargot only takes place at your local grocery store.

½ cup	double smoked bacon*, rind removed, diced	120 mL
½ cup	unsalted butter	120 mL
2	cloves garlic, minced	2
1	medium onion, diced	1
1	carrot, diced	1
1	celery stalk, diced	1
1	potato, peeled and diced	1
½ cup	flour	120 mL
6 cups	Chicken, Fish, or Vegetable Stock (pages 20–23)	1.5 L
1	bay leaf	1
2	3½ oz. (115-g) cans escargot	2
2 cups	frozen corn niblets	480 mL
2 cups	35% cream, warmed	480 mL
½ cup	pearl barley, blanched tender	120 mL
¼ cup	sliced fresh tarragon	60 mL
¼ cup	chopped fresh parsley	60 mL
	*See Glossary, page 202.	

In a stockpot on medium-high, cook the bacon for 3 minutes, until trans-lucent. Add the butter and sweat off the garlic, onions, carrot, celery, and potato for 5 minutes. There should be no browning of the vegetables, so don't cook on high heat. Dust with flour and mix well. Add the stock and bay leaf and keep stirring so the flour doesn't stick to the bottom of the pot and burn. Simmer 30 minutes. Add the escargot and corn and simmer for 5 minutes until the corn is tender. Remove the bay leaf and add the cream and barley and continue to simmer. Taste and adjust the seasonings. Just before serving, add the tarragon and parsley.

Olaf's Tip: Slightly warm up the cream before adding it to the soup mixture. Cold cream doesn't react well to hot liquids. Prepare soups the day before your event and store in the refrigerator. This allows the flavors to marry, enhancing the appeal of the soup.

Signature Cream of Roast Garlic Soup

Makes 12 cups (3 L)

This is a tried and true recipe. It is one of the signature dishes of our "On The Curve" Hot Stove and Wine Bar, in Mississauga, Ontario, and one to be treasured. If you're feeling tired, make up a batch of this; it's a sure-fire cure. And it's even better the next day. It sounds like the garlic might overwhelm your taste buds (and breath), but there's really just a soft hint of it when combined with potatoes and cream.

¼ cup	olive oil	60 mL
10	cloves garlic, peeled	10
2	medium onions, diced	2
2	sprigs fresh thyme, chopped	2
¼ cup	unsalted butter	60 mL
¼ cup	flour	60 mL
8 cups	Chicken or Vegetable Stock (pages 21 and 23)	2 L
2	medium Yukon Gold potatoes, peeled and diced	2
1	bay leaf	1
	salt and white pepper to taste	
2 cups	35% cream, warmed	480 mL

In a large, heavy pot or stockpot, heat the olive oil and sauté the garlic until golden brown. Add the onions, thyme, and butter. Continue to sauté for 5 minutes until tender. Dust with flour, mix well, and then add the stock, stirring constantly. Add the potatoes and bay leaf and simmer for 30 minutes. Remove the bay leaf, taste the stock, and add seasonings. Add the cream and purée in a food processor, blender, or with a hand blender. Strain through a fine mesh strainer into a pot, taste again, and adjust seasonings if necessary.

Garnish

¼ cup	unsalted butter	60 mL
1	clove garlic, minced	1
1 cup	rye bread cubes	240 mL
	salt and white pepper to taste	
1 cup	35% cream, whipped	240 mL
½ cup	sliced fresh chives	120 mL

In a frying pan over medium heat, melt the butter and sauté the garlic. Add the rye cubes and toast until crispy. Remove from the pan to paper towels. Season. Serve the soup steaming hot and garnish with the seasoned cubes/croutons, a dollop of whipped cream, and the chives.

Olaf's Tip: Whenever you are using a food processor or blender to purée a hot mixture, be very aware that the steam could cause the lid to pop off. A hand blender or mixer can also cause some serious burns if the hot soup splashes up. Allowing the hot mixture to cool slightly before blending reduces the danger. Also, use an oven mitt or heavy tea towel to hold the lid on while blending.

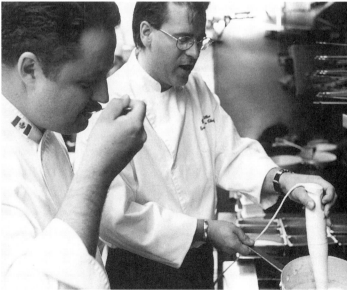

Duck Orange Punch

Serves 4

Are you up to a challenge? Do you want to sit down to a back-patting experience? This soup has been twisted to a punch-like combination of flavors with the addition of red wine and orange juice. The Asian twist gives a definite wow factor! Barbecued duck can by purchased at any Asian/Chinese marketplace. One of the more technically challenging dishes in this book, the chicken raft is tricky but it just needs time, patience, and supervision. While watching the raft form, prepare the garnishes. Then just sit back and inhale the rich flavors.

½	barbecued duck, deboned	½
16 cups	Chicken or Duck Stock (pages 21 and 22), or store-purchased	4 L
2 cups	red wine	480 mL
4 cups	orange juice	960 mL
1	clove garlic, chopped	1
2	cracked juniper berries	2
2	whole cloves	2
1	cinnamon stick	1
1	bay leaf	1
1 lb.	ground chicken meat	455 g
2 cups	diced onions	480 mL
2 cups	diced celery	480 mL
2 cups	diced carrots	480 mL
8	egg whites	8

Remove all the meat from the duck. Shred the meat and set aside.

In a stockpot or large, heavy pot, slowly simmer the barbecued duck bones, duck or chicken stock, red wine, orange juice, garlic, juniper berries, cloves, cinnamon stick, and bay leaf until reduced to 16 cups (4 L), then refrigerate until cold.

To the chilled stock add the ground chicken, onion, celery, carrots, and egg whites. Place over medium heat and stir frequently so that none of this mixture sticks to the bottom of the pot. After 10–15 minutes, this mixture will slowly come together and make a cake-like loaf that will float to the surface of the pot just like a raft. Simmer for 60 minutes. Remove from heat and, carefully, with a sharp knife, make a hole through the center of the floating raft big enough for your soup ladle to fit through. Without breaking the float, which would cause the broth to cloud, ladle out the broth into a clean pot. Drain the last of the broth through a fine strainer lined with cheesecloth and discard the raft. What is left is the makings of an amazing broth.

Olaf's Tip: Juniper berries can be found in most supermarkets, or the very least, gourmet specialty shops. This pungent spice is used to make gin!

The egg whites are necessary to hold the ground chicken and vegetables together and act as a sponge to gather the impurities and help keep a clear soup.

Garnishes

1 cup	pearl onions	240 mL
1	leek, julienned	1
1	carrot, julienned	1
1	shredded duck (as prepared earlier)	1
1 cup	Enoki mushrooms	240 mL

Blanch the pearl onions, leek, and carrot in boiling water for a minute. Quickly drain and put into an ice bath to stop the cooking process. Dry on paper towel. Divide the garnishes into warmed bowls and pour the hot punch over them.

Olaf's Tip: As the raft is forming, give the pot your full attention.

Leek, Corn, and Stilton Chowder

Serves 4

This is a soup to be served after a brisk autumn walk or after a day spent in the winter wonderland. The combination of sweet corn and blue cheese is extraordinary!

½ cup	vegetable oil	120 mL
1	onion, diced	1
2	large leeks, white only, diced	2
4	celery stalks, diced	4
3	fresh corn cobs, husked* or 2 cups (480 mL) frozen corn niblets	3
½ cup	unsalted butter	120 mL
½ cup	flour	120 mL
6 cups	Chicken or Vegetable Stock (pages 21 and 23), or store-purchased	1.5 L
1	bay leaf	1
2	large Yukon Gold potatoes, peeled, diced in ½-inch (1.2-cm) cubes	2
2 cups	35% cream	480 mL
	salt and pepper to taste	
1 cup	crumbled Stilton or Ermite blue cheese	240 mL
½ cup	coarsely chopped fresh parsley	120 mL

*If using fresh corn on the cob, use a very sharp knife to slice down the cob to remove the kernels.

In a medium-sized pot over medium heat, add the vegetable oil and sweat off the onions, leek, celery, and corn niblets for about 3–5 minutes. Add the butter and sauté for 2 minutes. Add the flour and mix quickly. Pour in the stock, add the bay leaf and stir constantly until the flour and broth are completely combined. Simmer for 30 minutes, but watch that pot. A thick chowder can burn very quickly.

Add the potatoes and simmer until tender. Add the cream and seasonings and simmer for 15 minutes more. Just before serving, fold in the cheese and chopped parsley. Check seasonings.

Olaf's Tip: A chowder always tastes better the next day, so plan this ahead. For an all-in-one meal, add diced smoked chicken.

Herbal Chicken "Cappuccino"
with Smoked Turkey Lentil Cake

Serves 4

If I were a doctor, this soup would be my herbal remedy for the common cold. Its hot liquid and flavors will blow your senses! The soup is very creamy and frothy, like cappuccino, so the cake hidden below the froth surprises all!

Part 1: The Soup

2	sprigs fresh chives	2
2	sprigs fresh dill	2
2	sprigs fresh basil	2
2	sprigs thyme	2
2	sprigs tarragon	2
¼ cup	unsalted butter	60 mL
3	cloves garlic, chopped	3
1	leek, white only, chopped	1
2	medium onions, diced	2
2	medium Yukon Gold potatoes, peeled and diced	2
1	bay leaf	1
¼ cup	flour	60 mL
6 cups	Chicken or Vegetable Stock (page 21 or 23), or store-purchased	1.5 L
1 cup	35% cream	240 mL
	salt and pepper to taste	
1 cup	mixed herbs (chives, dill, basil, thyme, tarragon)	240 mL
1 cup	chopped fresh parsley	240 mL
1 cup	chopped fresh spinach	240 mL
1 cup	35% cream, whipped	240 mL

Take 1 stem of each herb and tie them into a bundle. With the remaining stems, take off the leaves and mix them together to make 1 cup (240 mL).

In a stockpot or wide, heavy-bottomed pot, melt the butter and sweat off the garlic, leek, onions, potatoes, and bay leaf. Add the flour and mix well. Don't let the flour settle on the bottom of the pot. Add the cold stock, the herb bundle, and the liquid cream and simmer for 30 minutes. Remove the herb bundle and bay leaf and add seasonings. In a blender or food processor, mix in the remaining cup of mixed herbs, the parsley, and the spinach. Then just before serving, fold in the whipped cream to get the cappuccino effect. Set aside and keep warm while you prepare the lentil cake.

Part 2: Lentil Cake

2 Tbsp.	vegetable oil	30 mL
1	leek, finely chopped	1
1	onion, finely diced	1
1	red pepper, diced	1
2 Tbsp.	chopped fresh parsley	30 mL
1 lb.	smoked turkey, shredded	455 g
½ cup	red lentils, blanched until tender	120 mL
3	large egg yolks	3
¼ cup	cracker crumbs, your choice	60 mL
	salt and black pepper to taste	

Preheat the oven to 350°F (175°C). In a medium pan, sauté the leek, onion, and pepper until wilted. Transfer to a bowl and add the parsley, turkey, and red lentils together with the egg yolks. Add the cracker crumbs and season well. Form little burger-type patties and place on a baking sheet either greased or lined with parchment. Bake for 6 minutes.

To serve, place a warm lentil cake in the middle of a large soup bowl and pour the green frothy herbal soup around the cake.

 Olaf's Tip: The turkey–lentil mixture should be warm to allow the egg yolks to bind the ingredients together. To use as an herbal remedy, hang your head over the steam and inhale.

White Tomato Mousse

Serves 4

This dish provides a culinary illusion—your eyes are feasting on light, white fluffy mousse, but your tongue is tasting a tomato flavor so intense that you'll need only a small serving to make a big impression.

10	very ripe vine tomatoes	10
1/8 cup	gin	30 mL
5	leaves fresh basil	5
1/8 cup	red wine vinegar	30 mL
1/2	lemon, juice of	1/2
1/8 cup	sugar	30 mL
1 tsp.	salt	5 mL
	cayenne pepper to taste	
8	sheets gelatin	8
1/2 cup	35% cream, whipped	120 mL

Place the first eight ingredients in a food processor and coarsely chop. Place in a double cheesecloth and let hang over a bowl overnight.

Soak the gelatin in cold water, then remove any soft gelatin from the water. Take approximately 4 cups (960 mL) of the white tomato water and slightly warm it up. Remove from the heat and add the soft gelatin sheets. Whisk together. When this mixture has reached room temperature, fold in the whipped cream. Pour into molds, champagne flutes, or martini or parfait glasses. Chill for 1 hour or until set.

 Olaf's Tip: Use only very ripe tomatoes.

Serves 4

A table on the patio please! This is one of my signature salads. It's a summer salad with greens, grapefruit, and shrimp, with an incredibly light avocado mousse surprise. Get creative with the presentation by using interesting molds or bowls to shape your mousse, then surround it with the salad and shrimp.

4	sheets gelatin	4
1	ripe avocado, peeled and coarsely chopped	1
¼ cup	35% cream	60 mL
1	lime, juice of	1
1 cup	35% cream, whipped	240 mL
	salt and white pepper to taste	
4	handfuls mixed salad greens	4
2	pink grapefruits, peeled, in segments	2
12	fresh jumbo shrimp	12

Soak the gelatin sheets in cold water and set aside. In a food processor, combine the avocado, the ¼ cup (60 mL) of cream, and the lime juice. Remove the gelatin from the cold water and place in a small pan over medium heat. Melt the gelatin until liquid, then fold into the avocado purée until well mixed. Fold in the whipped cream. Add the seasonings. Pour into a large bowl or glasses and chill for 1 hour.

Peel the fresh shrimp and make a small cut from the tail of the shrimp to the other end. Remove the dark vein, toss the shrimp in a bowl with salt and pepper, and grill for 2 minutes per side on a hot barbecue.

Presentation: If chilled in a large bowl, scoop the mousse onto a chilled plate and garnish with the salad greens, pink grapefruit segments, and shrimp. You can also garnish the foam in individual glasses by decorating the rims with grapefruit segments or shrimps.

 Olaf's Tip: Do not make this dish too long before serving to prevent browning of the avocados. Prepare just a few hours before your guests arrive.

Warm Courses and Small Meals

These warm courses and small meals feel very personal to me. Most of these dishes were cooked for me by my grandmothers and are strongly embedded in my memory. The strength of my Omas' cooking gave me the foundation for my own food passions.

Some of these meals are comfort foods or "all-in-one" meals. There's nothing like slowly stewed brews or handmade pastas. Comfort foods suit chefs just fine since they are usually very easy to serve, with all the food groups in one dish.

With meals like this, a lot of flavors come together in one easy-to-eat dish, and they usually feature inexpensive ingredients. Some of the traditional dishes offered here have a real history and depth, because they were created and fine-tuned by centuries of testing. They have some set ingredients that must be included, but remember—all presentation rules are meant to be broken!

With the slow cooking over a long period of time, the final taste, flavors, and textures can only be described as "wow"!

Serves 4

This dish is well worth the effort. Your guests will be amazed at the flavor of roast duck and the White Wine and Lemon Butter Sauce, page 26. You can use the Ravioli Dough recipe, page 37. Chicken legs and thighs can be substituted for the duck.

Part 1: Duck Leg Preparation

1 lb.	unsalted butter	455 g
2 cups	vegetable oil	480 mL
2	bay leaves	2
1 Tbsp.	kosher salt	15 mL
4	duck legs with thigh attached	4

Heat the butter, oil, and bay leaves over medium heat in a pot deep enough to lay the duck legs on the bottom. Slowly simmer for about 45–60 minutes until tender, turning halfway through the cooking time. The meat should easily flake off the bone and the skin should be a golden brown color. Remove from the pot, cool, and then pull the skin and meat off the bones. Roughly cut the meat into ¼-inch (.6-cm) pieces. Do the same for the skin. Set aside until ready to add to the stuffing mixture.

Olaf's Tip: I love to use kosher salt for these duck legs because it cures the leg meat by penetrating the flesh and leaving a slightly salty texture.

continued on next page

Part 2: Ravioli Stuffing

1/3 cup	unsalted butter	80 mL
2 cups	finely diced leek	480 mL
1 cup	finely diced onion	240 mL
2	green onions, finely sliced	2
1/4 cup	chopped fresh parsley	60 mL
2 Tbsp.	chopped fresh rosemary	30 mL
2 Tbsp.	chopped fresh thyme	30 mL
	duck legs, prepared as above	
2	egg yolks	2
	salt and black pepper to taste	
1 cup	dry bread crumbs	240 mL
1 recipe	Ravioli Dough (page 37) (or 8 won ton wrappers, store-purchased)	1 recipe
1	egg, beaten	1
1/4 cup	milk	60 mL
1 recipe	White Wine and Lemon Butter Sauce (page 26)	1 recipe

In a pan, melt the butter and add the leek and onions. Sauté until the vegetables are tender. Add the herbs and roughly a quarter of the duck meat. Mix well. Place mixture into a bowl and, while still warm, add the egg yolks. Season and mix. Using a hand blender or food processor, quickly blend for a few seconds, leaving the mixture chunky. Don't overblend; just enough to mix the egg well. You want to keep the chunks of duck visible. Add the remaining shredded duck meat and the bread crumbs and using your hands, mix the ingredients thoroughly. This should be dry but somewhat sticky to the touch. Let the mixture cool.

At this point, prepare the White Wine and Lemon Butter Sauce, page 26.

Cut the ravioli dough into 4-inch (10-cm) squares. You will need 8 squares in total. Make a mound of about 3 Tbsp. (45 mL) of the stuffing mixture in the center of the ravioli squares. Make an egg wash with the egg and milk and cover the perimeter of the squares. Cover with another sheet of ravioli dough and seal firmly with a scalloped pastry roller or your fingers. When ready to serve, blanch the ravioli in boiling salted water for 3 minutes until tender.

Part 3: Buttered Squash Garnish

1	small squash, peeled, seeded, and finely diced	1
½ cup	raisins	120 mL
4 Tbsp.	unsalted butter	60 mL
1 oz.	Frangelico liqueur	28 g
	salt and white pepper to taste	
1 Tbsp.	chopped fresh parsley	15 mL

Over medium heat, sauté the squash and raisins to slightly char the squash pieces. Add the butter and liqueur. Simmer until the squash is tender. Add the seasonings and toss in the parsley.

Presentation: Pool the sauce to form a circle in the middle of a warmed serving plate, place the ravioli in a ring around the sauce and fill in the center with the Buttered Squash Garnish.

Stuttgart Ravioli

Serves 4 for a main course or more as a pasta course

This hot, rich chicken-broth base with hearty meat-and-cheese-stuffed ravioli is a great way to beat the chill of a cool day. It's a wonderful way to jazz up a simple family meal—even your kids will enjoy this one!

Part 1: Ravioli Stuffing

¼ cup	vegetable oil	60 mL
1	small onion, finely diced	1
1	clove garlic, minced	1
¼ lb.	each of ground pork and ground beef	113 g
1 cup	frozen spinach, thawed, drained, and chopped	240 mL
½ cup	grated Swiss Emmenthal cheese	120 mL
2 Tbsp.	fresh white bread crumbs*	30 mL
2	large egg yolks	2
2 Tbsp.	chopped fresh parsley	30 mL
	salt and black pepper to taste	
	*See Glossary, page 202.	

In a large pan, heat oil over medium heat. Sauté the onions, garlic, and meats until cooked through. Drain off any excess oil. Add the remaining ingredients. This mixture should be dry but tacky to the touch. Chill in the refrigerator while you make the ravioli dough.

Part 2: Ravioli

1 recipe	Ravioli Dough (page 37)	1 recipe
1	large egg	1
¼ cup	milk	60 mL
1 cup	cornmeal	240 mL

Cut forty 2-inch (5-cm) squares of ravioli dough and egg-wash the edges with the mixed egg and milk. Place approximately 1 heaping teaspoon (5 mL) of filling in the center of each ravioli square. Place another ravioli square on top. Seal in the filling with a scalloped pastry roller or with your fingers. Place on a cookie sheet lightly dusted with cornmeal. (These can be frozen for 2 months or refrigerated for 4 days.)

Part 3: Broth

| 6 cups | Chicken Stock (page 21), or store-purchased | 1.5 L |
| 2 Tbsp. | cold unsalted butter, cubed | 30 mL |

Place the stock in a pot and bring to a slow boil. Cook the ravioli in the broth for 3 minutes until tender. Spoon the finished ravioli into large soup or pasta bowls and set aside. Whisk the cold butter cubes into the hot broth. Keep the broth warm while you prepare the garnish.

Part 4: Garnish

⅓ cup	vegetable oil	80 mL
1 Tbsp.	unsalted butter	15 mL
2	medium onions, sliced	2
2 Tbsp.	chopped fresh chives	30 mL
2 Tbsp.	chopped fresh parsley	30 mL

In a medium pan, heat the oil and butter and sauté the onions until a crispy golden brown. Set aside.

Presentation: Pour the hot broth over the ravioli in each bowl and top with roasted onions. Garnish with the chives and parsley.

Olaf's Tip: Make sure the ravioli mixture is dry but tacky to the touch. If the bread crumbs are too wet, the ravioli might burst open. If you're really rushed for time, try won ton wrappers (available from most grocery stores) instead of ravioli.

Risotto for the First-Timer

Serves 4

This is a basic but delicious comfort food. It's a great one to prepare while your guests are nearly ready to sit down. The aromas that fill your kitchen as this simmers on your stove will have your guests chomping at the bit! Give them a glass of wine and let their mouths water while they wait.

2 Tbsp.	olive oil	30 mL
1	onion, finely diced	1
1 cup	arborio rice	240 mL
¾ cup	white wine	180 mL
4 cups	Chicken or Vegetable Stock (pages 21 and 23), or store-purchased	960 mL
⅓ cup	unsalted butter	80 mL
⅓ cup	35% cream	80 mL
⅓ cup	Parmesan cheese	80 mL
	salt and white pepper to taste	

In a large pot, heat the olive oil and sweat off the onion until translucent. Add the rice and quickly sauté. Deglaze with the white wine and reduce by 90%, about 3–5 minutes. Add 1 cup (240 mL) of the stock and stir, keeping the rice grains from sticking. When the rice has absorbed the stock in the pot, about 3–5 minutes, add another cup (240 mL) of stock and continue stirring. Keep adding stock and stirring until the stock is all used and the rice has a very soft texture, but is still al dente. Add the butter, cream, and cheese. Add the seasonings. Serve immediately.

 Olaf's Tip: This can be a great vegetarian dish. Add your choice of vegetables at the end and cook until they are just crunchy. By adding ingredients, you can make this dish as complicated or as simple as you wish—see the following recipe for more ideas. It may be a new way to use up Sunday leftovers: Risotto Mondays!

Tomato Trilogy Risotto

Serves 4

The adaptations for risotto are endless! A few twists to my basic risotto change the flavor completely. There are no boundaries—seafood, chicken, beef, or pork pieces, any and all vegetables, diced, julienned, sliced! It's a great way to use leftovers. Make up a Salad from the Market, page 55, and supper is ready. This recipe uses three varieties of tomatoes to give a fantastic fresh taste.

1 cup	halved grape or cherry tomatoes	240 mL
¼ cup	chopped sun-dried tomatoes (see Tip)	60 mL
3 cups	chopped Italian plum tomatoes	720 mL
1 recipe	Risotto for the First-Timer (page 86)	1 recipe
8	fresh basil leaves, chopped	8

Mix the tomatoes together. Following the Risotto for the First-Timer recipe on the previous page, add the tomato mixture to the rice after the wine reduction. Continue with the risotto instructions, adding the stock until absorbed but with the rice still al dente. Just before serving, add the chopped basil.

Olaf's Tip: If using dry sun-dried tomatoes (as opposed to those packed in oil), soak them in 2 cups (480 mL) of water for at least 2 hours before making this dish. Remove the softened tomatoes from the water. You might want to use this water in the risotto—just replace the stock with equal amounts of the water. Oil-packed sun-dried tomatoes can also be used. They won't need to be soaked since they are already tender and moist.

Butternut Squash Risotto
with Pistachio and Smoked Turkey

Serves 4

This is a "twist" on Thanksgiving dinner—an "all-in-one" feast! This risotto
has been made into a very hearty main course with the addition of butter-
nut squash and turkey. Once you see how easy it is to do, you can add
your own "twists" with flavors you choose.

¼ lb.	unsalted butter	113 g
1	small white onion, finely diced	1
1 cup	whole pistachios, shelled	240 mL
1½ cups	arborio rice	360 mL
2 cups	white wine	480 mL
1 tsp.	saffron	5 mL
2 cups	butternut squash, cut into small cubes	480 mL
5 cups	Chicken Stock (page 21), or store-purchased	1.2 L
1 lb.	smoked turkey, small cubes (see Tip)	455 g
1 cup	35% cream	240 mL
½ cup	Parmesan cheese	120 mL
¼ cup	chopped fresh parsley	60 mL
	salt and white pepper to taste	

Melt the butter and sauté the onions, pistachios, and rice for 5 minutes.
Deglaze with the white wine and saffron and reduce by 90%. Add the
squash and then start adding the chicken stock a cup (240 mL) at a time,
stirring constantly, until absorbed by the rice. Add the smoked turkey.
When the stock is all absorbed the rice should be al dente. Finish off
with the cream, cheese, and parsley.

Add the seasonings before serving.

Garnish

| 2 cups | port wine | 480 mL |
| 1 cup | dried cranberries | 240 mL |

In a small pot, toss the cranberries into the port wine, simmer and reduce by 50%, until it is a thick, syrup-like consistency.

Presentation: To serve, mound the finished risotto in the middle of warm plates and drizzle the cranberry and port wine syrup around the risotto.

Olaf's Tip: When cooking arborio rice, adding white wine will give you a much more tender grain.

Ask a good deli to cut a smoked turkey breast into ½-inch (1.2-cm) slices. Some delis sell a whole smoked turkey thigh that you can then cut yourself. Once you cook with smoked meats, you will notice an immediate difference in flavor. Nothing can replace that taste.

Mushroom and Cheese Soufflé

Serves 4

This isn't a classic soufflé, but it tastes like one. You can't fail with this type of soufflé. It has a crispy marshmallow-type texture and it won't sink like you imagine soufflés do. This is a great make-ahead dish that allows you to change the ingredients to suit your pantry or tastes. Remove the cheddar cheese and substitute other cheese to achieve a different taste. Replace the mushrooms with your choice of vegetables or herbs. This recipe is limitless in flavor opportunities.

Part 1: Mushrooms

1 cup	olive oil	240 mL
½ lb.	mushrooms, mixed variety, finely chopped	225 g
⅓ cup	unsalted butter	80 mL
2 Tbsp.	finely diced shallots or onions	30 mL
½	lemon, juice of	½
2 Tbsp.	finely chopped fresh parsley	30 mL

In a large frying pan, heat the oil and sauté the mushrooms until golden brown. Add the butter and shallots or onions and sauté until translucent. Squeeze in the lemon juice and add the parsley. Set aside to cool.

Part 2: Soufflé

2	large egg whites, whipped to peaks	2
1 cup	unsalted butter	240 mL
1	small onion, finely diced	1
1 cup	flour	240 mL
3 cups	whole milk	720 mL
1	bay leaf	1
	salt and white pepper to taste	
	mushrooms (as prepared previously)	
2	large egg yolks, beaten	2
1 cup	grated aged white cheddar cheese	240 mL
	unsalted butter for greasing the dishes	
	flour for dusting the dishes	

Prepare the egg whites and refrigerate until ready to use.

In a large pan, melt the butter and sweat off the onions until translucent. Add the flour and quickly stir in the milk. Add the bay leaf and simmer for 15 minutes until the mixture thickens. Taste and season. Pour this mixture through a fine mesh strainer to remove any lumps. Combine the mushrooms into the creamy sauce. While this mixture is still warm, fold in the egg yolks and grated cheese. Allow the mixture to cool to room temperature, then fold in the chilled egg whites.

Preheat the oven to 350°F (175°C). Get four ¾-cup (180-mL) ramekin dishes and grease the insides completely with butter, then dust with flour. Fill the dishes ¾ full with the prepared mixture and place in a water bath (see Tip). Poach for 30–45 minutes or until firm to the touch and light brown on top. Run a warm knife around the ramekin dishes and unmold onto warm plates.

Olaf's Tip: A water bath? Take a 3-inch (7.5-cm) high lasagna pan or other baking pan and place the prepared ramekin dishes in the pan. Place the pan in the oven and then add the hot water nearly to the top of the dishes. This way there's no balancing act to get the water-filled pan into the oven. Likewise, remove the cooked ramekins from the hot water bath while the pan's still in the oven so that the water doesn't scald you or splash into the cooked soufflé.

I chose to use individual ramekin dishes for this recipe to bring the cooking time to a minimum while you are entertaining. If you do make one large soufflé, it will take 45–60 minutes or until firm to the touch.

Chicken Cacciatore

Serves 4

There is no substitute for this basic Italian country cooking style. Serve this dish with crusty bread, a glass of red wine, and don't forget the checkered tablecloth.

1	whole chicken, 2–3 lbs. (.9–1.35 kg) or 8 pieces of chicken, your choice, but must have bone in and skin on!	1
	salt and pepper	
	flour for coating the chicken	
1 cup	olive oil	240 mL
1	medium onion, cut into 8	1
2	cloves garlic, minced	2
½ cup	tomato paste	120 mL
3 cups	red wine	720 mL
2 cups	Chicken Stock (page 21), or store-purchased	480 mL
4 cups	plum tomatoes, with juice	960 mL
4	sprigs fresh basil, half chopped, and half in fine strips	2
1	sprig fresh oregano, chopped	1
1	sprig fresh thyme, chopped	1
1	lemon, zest of	1
1	each of red and yellow pepper	1
1	red onion, cut into rings	1
2	large portobello mushrooms, cut in quarters	2

Preheat the oven to 450°F (230°C). Cut the whole chicken into eight pieces, season well with salt and pepper, and lightly coat with flour. On medium heat, heat the oil in a braising pan or ovenproof pan and roast the chicken pieces until brown. Add the onions and garlic and continue frying until golden brown. Add the tomato paste. Roast 3–5 minutes to cook out the bitter particles. Add 1 cup (240 mL) of the red wine and reduce 80% of the liquid. Repeat twice more. Add the chicken stock and diced plum tomatoes with juice. Add the oregano, thyme, lemon zest, and the chopped basil. Cover and simmer in the oven for 30–45 minutes.

Chop the peppers into 2-inch (5-cm) pieces. In the last 10 minutes of cooking the chicken and sauce, add the peppers, red onion, and mushrooms. Mix the fine strips of basil into the sauce. Taste and adjust the seasonings if necessary. This will refrigerate well for 3–5 days. Can be frozen for up to 1 month.

Olaf's Tip: Leaving the bones in the chicken makes this dish juicer. This dish can be frozen.

Chicken Fricassée

Serves 4

This dish is an old country favorite from Germany and is one of the first
dishes my father taught me to cook. It's a creamy chicken stew that will
really warm your soul!

5¼ cups	Chicken Stock (page 21), or store-purchased	1.25 L
4	5-oz. (140-g) chicken breasts, boneless, skinless	4
1 lb.	fresh asparagus spears, cut into ½-inch (1.2-cm) pieces	455 g
3 Tbsp.	unsalted butter	45 mL
4 Tbsp.	flour	60 mL
¾ cup	whole milk	180 mL
⅓ cup	35% cream	80 mL
½ tsp.	salt	2.5 mL
¼ tsp.	white pepper	1.2 mL
¼ cup	capers, drained	60 mL
1 cup	pre-cooked frozen crawfish or baby shrimp, thawed	240 mL
1 cup	sliced shiitake mushrooms	240 mL
1	sweet red pepper, 1-inch (2.5-cm) circles	1
1	sweet yellow pepper, 1-inch (2.5-cm) circles	1
1 cup	sour cream	240 mL
1 Tbsp.	chopped fresh dill	15 mL

In 4 cups (950 mL) of stock, poach the chicken breasts for 12–15 minutes until done. Remove from heat and dice into ½-inch (1.2-cm) pieces. In another pot, cook the asparagus in salted water for 2–4 minutes until just tender. Refresh asparagus under cold water to stop the cooking process. Slice into ½-inch (1.2-cm) pieces.

In a medium pot on low heat, melt the butter. Stir in the flour to make a roux. Whisk in the remaining 1¼ cups (300 mL) chicken stock slowly and continue stirring until smooth. Whisk in the milk, then the cream. Increase heat to medium and continue stirring until the mixture thickens. Reduce heat to simmer for 30 minutes. At this point, the sauce should be quite thick. Season with salt and white pepper. Remove from heat and strain through a mesh strainer to get rid of any lumps. Fold in the chicken pieces, asparagus, capers, crawfish or shrimp, mushrooms, and peppers. Taste and adjust seasoning if necessary. To refine the flavor, add the sour cream and the dill. Serve over rice, fresh pasta, or potato gnocchi. This will refrigerate well for 3 days. Can be frozen for up to 1 month.

Olaf's Tip: When adding the chicken stock into the flour, make sure the flour is warm and the stock is cold. It's also important to stir constantly to avoid lumps. If the mixture does get lumpy, strain through a sieve and continue with the recipe. Check your local grocery store's frozen fish counter for crawfish, or at gourmet stores or fish markets.

Penne Noodles with Chicken
in Roast Garlic Butter Broth

Serves 4

If you like chicken noodle soup, then you will want to make this rich, light pasta creation.

1½ lbs.	fresh penne pasta, or 1 lb. (455 g) dry penne pasta	680 g
½ cup	olive oil	120 mL
2	chicken breasts, boneless, skinless, cut in ½-inch (1.2-cm) strips	2
2	cloves garlic, minced	2
2 cups	sliced mushrooms	480 mL
2	large Roma tomatoes, coarsely chopped	2
½ cup	dry white wine	120 mL
2 cups	Chicken Stock (page 21), or store-purchased	480 mL
½ cup	cold butter, cubed	120 mL
½ cup	grated Parmesan cheese	120 mL
2 Tbsp.	chopped fresh parsley	30 mL
	salt and black pepper to taste	

In a large pot of boiling salted water, cook the fresh penne pasta for about 5 minutes or until al dente. For the dry pasta, follow the directions on the package. Drain off the water.

In a large frying pan over medium heat, heat the oil and sear the chicken strips for about 5 minutes, browning on all sides. Remove the chicken and set aside.

In the same pan, sauté the minced garlic and mushrooms until light brown. Add the tomatoes and cook for 3 minutes. Deglaze with the white wine and simmer until the wine has completely evaporated. Add the chicken stock and bring to a boil. Remove from the heat and whisk in the cubes of butter. Return the chicken pieces to the pan, add the penne, cheese, and parsley. Add the seasonings.

Olaf's Tip: When you cook the pasta to al dente and drain off the water, place the pasta onto an oiled tray. Don't rinse the hot pasta with cold water as this will remove the fine layer of sticky starch needed to help the sauce stick to each noodle.

Fettuccine with a Creamy Seafood and Basil Stew

Serves 4

When you are visiting with your guests and it comes time for you to slip into the kitchen to throw something together—this is the dish! Quick, easy, and everything ready to go!

1½ lbs.	fresh fettuccine pasta, or 1 lb. (455 g) dry fettuccine pasta	680 g
3 Tbsp.	olive oil	45 mL
8	jumbo shrimp	8
8	jumbo scallops	8
	salt and white pepper to taste	
2	cloves garlic, minced	2
2 Tbsp.	unsalted butter	30 mL
2 Tbsp.	flour	30 mL
1½ cups	dry white wine	360 mL
2 cups	35% cream	480 mL
½	lemon, finely grated zest and juice	½
1	red pepper, cut in strips	1
2	sprigs fresh basil, chopped	2
12 oz.	canned lobster meat, drained	340 mL
	salt and white pepper to taste	
	chopped fresh basil or parsley for garnish	

In a large pot of boiled salted water, cook the fresh penne for about 5 minutes or until al dente. For the dry penne, follow the directions on the package. Drain off the water.

In a large frying pan over medium-high heat, heat the oil and sauté the shrimps and scallops for 2 minutes. With a slotted spoon, remove the seafood from the pan, drain onto a paper towel, and season well.

In the same pan, sauté the garlic until lightly browned. Stir in the butter until melted and whisk in the flour to make a smooth paste. Cook for a minute, then whisk in the wine. Add the cream, lemon zest, and juice and simmer gently for 5 minutes. Fold in the pepper, basil, lobster meat, and the shrimp and scallops. Add seasonings. Toss in the penne and simmer just long enough to heat the pasta. Serve immediately.

Presentation: When making individual servings or even on a large platter, make sure the plates or bowls are warm. To serve any pasta with precious seafoods, twist a mound of noodles and top with the seafood. Garnish with a sprinkling of chopped basil or parsley.

 Olaf's Tip: Don't overcook your seafood. It just needs a quick roasting and then remove from the pan until needed.

Fish Dishes

This chapter and the next (The Main Course) reflect my strengths. I got my interest in fish through my grandfather. On Fridays in Berlin, Opa loved to go to the market in the early morning for only the freshest of fish to be served for a hot lunch. The way the fish was to be prepared, the accompaniments, and the sauce that would marry it all together formed the topic for great discussion. This meal I was never late for!

The special treat was our trip to the world-famous KA DE WA Department Store in Berlin and the hours spent wandering on the top floor, which contained a huge gourmet food store. This gastronomical haven provided everything the world had to offer in foods and ingredients, and it also had several mini-restaurants. There was a standing-only restaurant and fish market that was always packed, about ten people deep, all lined up for a chat with the fishmonger. The market had all the fresh fish you could imagine, ready for you to take home or be prepared to perfection right there for your taste buds to savor. The fish was always served with very simple steamed new potatoes with parsley, a refreshing salad, and just the natural juices of the fish—it was unheard of to hide the flavors with any thick sauces or overpowering lemon juice.

This was my motivation for learning about this style of cooking which puts the fish at the forefront of taste, with the texture juicy and moist. The sauce and accompaniments are secondary; they are just accents for the fresh fish. I know you will love it too.

Serves 4

This is one of my signature dishes; it looks and tastes really impressive. I love onions in all variations, so Onions[3], using three different kinds of onions, makes this recipe three times better. When onions are served along with medium-rare salmon, they're amazing. This dish can be prepared in advance of your guests' arrival; you will need only about 10 minutes to prepare before serving.

Part 1: Red Onion and Mushroom Compote

2	small red onions, julienned	2
¼ cup	unsalted butter	60 mL
1 Tbsp.	sugar	15 mL
1½ cups	red wine	360 mL
1 cup	quartered shiitake mushrooms	240 mL
1 Tbsp.	chopped fresh thyme	15 mL
1 Tbsp.	chopped fresh tarragon	15 mL
	salt and white pepper to taste	

Sauté the red onions gently in butter until translucent. Add the sugar and cook until it is dissolved. Deglaze the pan with red wine and simmer gently until the liquid is reduced to a thick syrup, about 5 minutes. In a separate pan, sauté the mushrooms with the herbs. Mix into the red onions. Season with salt and pepper.

continued on next page

Part 2: Red Wine Foamy Sauce

½ cup	35% cream	120 mL
10	shallots, halved	10
¼ cup	unsalted butter	60 mL
¼ cup	white vinegar	60 mL
1 cup	red wine	240 mL
½ cup	cold unsalted butter, cubed	120 mL
	salt and white pepper to taste	

Whip the cream to stiff peaks and place in the refrigerator until needed. Char the shallots for about 3–5 minutes in a hot, dry pan. Let the pan cool to medium heat, then add the ¼ cup (60 mL) of butter and sauté. Add the white vinegar and reduce to a syrup. Deglaze with the red wine and reduce by ¾.

Put aside the sauce at this point and move on to Part 3. Finish this sauce just before serving. When you are ready to serve, take the sauce off the heat, whisk in the cold butter cubes until emulsified. Season to taste. Just before serving, fold in the whipped cream. Serve immediately.

Olaf's Tip: Using cold butter cubes when finishing the sauce is a thickening agent of sorts, but will work only if the butter is cold.

Part 3: Crispy Leeks Garnish

1	large whole leek	1
	vegetable oil for frying	
	salt and pepper to taste	

Wash and julienne the leek. Pat dry with a paper towel. Slowly heat the oil on the stove in a deep pot to 310°F (155°C) degrees. Fry the leek in the oil until golden brown. Remove from oil and dry on a paper towel and immediately season with salt and pepper. Set aside until ready to serve.

Part 4: The Salmon

4	6-oz. (170-g) fillets Atlantic salmon, center cut, scales removed, skin on	4
	salt and pepper to taste	
2 Tbsp.	olive oil	30 mL

Preheat the oven to 400°F (200°C). Season the salmon on both sides. In a hot pan with a little vegetable oil, sauté the fish with the skin facing up for about 2 minutes or until golden brown. Turn the fillet over so the skin side is down. If your pan is ovenproof, put the whole pan into the oven. If not, place the fish in a shallow pan and bake for 10 minutes or until the internal temperature reaches 145°F (60°C).

Presentation: Place the red onion and mushroom compote in the center of each plate with a salmon fillet on top. Place the shallots around the salmon and spoon the Red Wine Foamy Sauce around the red onion compote. Garnish with the crispy leeks.

 Olaf's Tip: This dish can be prepared well in advance to make entertaining easy. You can pre-sear the salmon, place on a baking sheet, and refrigerate until ready to bake. The red onion compote can be made ahead and warmed up. The foamy sauce can be pre-made to the point indicated in the recipe and warmed up when you're ready. You can deep-fry the leeks in advance and store in a dry, closed container.

Rainbow Trout with Red Wine Hollandaise

Serves 4

The secret to cooking rainbow trout is having the freshest possible product, cooking it quickly, and undercooking it slightly. This brings out the natural flavors and juices that this fish has to offer. I suggest combining this fish dish with my Warm Potato Salad, page 160. If calories are a concern, try the Lemon Caper Relish, page 158, instead of the hollandaise.

Part 1: Red Wine Hollandaise Sauce

1 Tbsp.	unsalted butter	15 mL
2	shallots, minced	2
1 tsp.	cracked black peppercorns	5 mL
1	bay leaf	1
3 Tbsp.	red wine vinegar	45 mL
1½ cups	red wine	360 mL
5	large egg yolks	5
¼ tsp.	cracked white pepper	1.2 mL
1 Tbsp.	Dijon mustard	15 mL
2 cups	clarified butter*	480 mL
½	lemon, juice of	½ each
	salt and white pepper to taste	
½ tsp.	cayenne pepper	2.5 mL

*See Glossary, page 202.

In a medium pan over high heat, add the butter and sauté the shallots, black peppercorns, and bay leaf until the shallots become translucent. Deglaze with the red wine vinegar and red wine and reduce by 90%. Strain the wine liquid into a bowl containing the egg yolks. Whisk the mixture over a double boiler (or a stainless steel bowl over a pot of simmering water) until the yolks form a ribbon or stick to the back of a spoon. Remove the bowl from the double boiler, add the Dijon mustard, and slowly whisk in the clarified butter a little at a time until emulsified. Flavor with the lemon juice, salt, white pepper, and cayenne. Pour into a clean container and place in a warm area.

Olaf's Tip: If the mixture gets too thick, add 1 Tbsp. (15 mL) of water until the desired consistency is reached. If it breaks or separates, whisk 3 large egg yolks and ½ cup (120 mL) of wine together and whisk over a double boiler until ribbons are formed. Remove from the heat and slowly whisk the broken mixture into the newly whisked egg yolks and wine.

Part 2: Rainbow Trout

4	small rainbow trout fillets	4
	salt and white pepper to taste	
1 Tbsp.	paprika	15 mL
1 cup	flour	240 mL
½ cup	olive oil	120 mL
1 Tbsp.	unsalted butter	15 mL
¼	lemon wedge	¼

Season the fillets with salt and pepper. Mix the paprika and flour and dredge the fillets in this mixture. Shake off the excess flour. Heat the olive oil and butter over a medium-high heat, add the lemon wedge, and carefully place the fillets into the pan. Roast until medium-rare to medium, about 5–7 minutes. Don't overcook. It should just flake apart. Remove from pan and pat off excess oil.

Olaf's Tip: The best way to judge the freshness of fish is to smell it. Always ask to smell the fish before buying it from your market or grocery counter. A "fishy" smell is a sign of age and indicates you should buy elsewhere. In my experience, Asian markets have the freshest possible fish.

New Age Fish and Chips
with a Chunky Citrus Tartar Sauce

Serves 4

This halibut and lemony sauce make "fish night" something very special. The chips, made from a variety of root vegetables, are a great way to get kids to eat their veggies. And don't spoil your supper by nibbling!

Part 1: Chunky Citrus Tartar Sauce

1 cup	sour cream	240 mL
1 cup	mayonnaise	240 mL
2 Tbsp.	green relish	30 mL
2	lemons, juice of	2
3 Tbsp.	finely chopped fresh parsley	45 mL
3 Tbsp.	finely chopped fresh chives	45 mL
¼ cup	small capers, drained	60 mL
¼ cup	finely diced black olives	60 mL
2	small tomatoes, finely diced	2
2 Tbsp.	chopped fresh tarragon	30 mL
1	small onion, finely diced	1
¼ cup	chopped fresh dill	60 mL
	salt and black pepper to taste	

In a bowl, whisk together the sour cream, mayonnaise, green relish, and lemon juice. Fold in the remaining vegetables and herbs. Taste and season. This should be made at least an hour or two ahead to give time for the flavors to marry.

Part 2: Root Vegetable Chips

1	Yukon Gold potato	1
1	Russet potato	1
1	parsnip	1
1	carrot	1
1	sweet potato	1
1	plantain, still green	1
1	lotus root	1
	oil for deep-frying	
	salt and white pepper to taste	

Use as many or as few of these kinds of root vegetables as you like. Peel and then slice paper thin—try a mandolin! Heat the oil to 310°F (155°C) and slowly deep-fry the vegetables, a few at a time, for approximately 1 minute, until golden brown and crispy. Remove to a paper towel to absorb any excess oil and, while still hot, season with salt and pepper. Be careful: the high sugar content in the carrots, parsnips, and sweet potatoes makes them easy to burn. Place in a warm oven to keep them warm, or store them in an airtight container and rewarm in a 350°F (175°C) oven for 5 minutes.

Part 3: The Halibut

4	6-oz. (170-g) halibut fillets, skinless	4
	salt and pepper to taste	
1 Tbsp.	paprika	15 mL
1 cup	flour	240 mL
1 cup	olive oil	240 mL
2 Tbsp.	unsalted butter	30 mL

Preheat the oven to 400°F (200°C). Season the halibut with the salt, pepper, and paprika to suit your own taste, then dredge in flour. Pat off any excess flour. In a large, ovenproof frying pan, heat the olive oil and sear the halibut about 2 minutes on one side. Add the butter and turn the fish over and cook the other side for about 2 minutes for a great texture and a crispy crust. Bake in the oven for 5 minutes or until it reaches an internal temperature of 140°F (60°C). Remove from the pan and pat off any excess oil.

Presentation: Mound a handful of chips onto each plate. Place the fish on the chips and top with a large dollop of tartar sauce.

 Olaf's Tip: If there are any leftover chips, store them in a dry closed container and use them for cocktailing or for lunch!

Potato and Basil-Crusted
Pickerel on a Cherry Tomato Dressing

Serves 4

Crusted, roasted white fish, vine-ripened tomatoes, and basil—this is such a terrific combination of flavors. For this all-in-one dish, you can substitute the pickerel with snapper, perch, cod, or haddock—your choice. The Cherry Tomato Dressing is also great for salads or with grilled chicken.

Part 1: Cherry Tomato Dressing

1 pint (2 cups)	cherry tomatoes	480 mL
½	small onion	½
1 Tbsp.	honey	15 mL
½ cup	white wine vinegar	120 mL
1 Tbsp.	Dijon mustard	15 mL
½	lemon, juice of	½
1 cup	olive oil	240 mL
	salt and white pepper to taste	

Place the tomatoes into a blender or food processor and add the rest of the ingredients, except the oil and seasonings. With the machine still running, slowly drizzle in the olive oil. Add the seasonings. Set aside.

Olaf's Tip: To make the dressing lighter, use half water and half oil, or Vegetable Stock, page 23.

Part 2: Potato Basil Crust

2	small Yukon Gold potatoes, peeled and sliced paper-thin	2
1	small onion, finely sliced	1
16	large fresh basil leaves, finely sliced	16
1	large egg yolk	1
	salt and black pepper to taste	

Toss the potatoes, onion, basil leaves, and egg yolk together and season well. Set aside.

Part 3: The Fish

4	6-oz. (170-g) pickerel portions	4
	salt and pepper to taste	
1 tsp.	paprika	5 mL
¼ cup	flour	60 mL
¼ cup	olive oil for frying	60 mL
2 Tbsp.	Dijon mustard	30 mL
2 Tbsp.	oil	30 mL
2 Tbsp.	unsalted butter	30 mL

Preheat the oven to 400°F (200°C). Season the fish with salt and pepper. Combine the paprika and flour on a plate and dredge the fish portions. Brush off any excess flour. Heat the oil in a non-stick frying pan and sear both sides of the pickerel but do not cook completely, about 1 minute on each side.

Brush the Dijon mustard on one side of the seared pickerel. Place a layer of the potato slices, with a few strands of onion in between. Press the potatoes into the mustard. Then, in a clean, ovenproof frying pan, heat the oil and butter and carefully place the pickerel into the pan, potato-side down. Place in the oven and slowly bake for about 10 minutes, or until the potato crust is a crispy golden brown and the fish is completely cooked. Remove from the pan and pat off excess oil.

Presentation: Pool the room-temperature Cherry Tomato Dressing onto warmed plates and place the fish, potato-side up, on top.

Arctic Char on Mussel Citrus Stew

Serves 4

Arctic Char is a truly great treat. The icy water of its habitat makes it a great textured fish that is clean and light, with a unique taste that has become a favorite with fish lovers.

Part 1: White Wine and Lemon Butter Sauce (page 26)

Part 2: Mussel Citrus Stew

1	small red pepper	1
1	small yellow pepper	1
1	small carrot	1
1	small green zucchini	1
1	small yellow zucchini	1
1	stalk celery	1
1 lb.	fresh cultivated mussels	455 g
2 Tbsp.	finely diced shallots	30 mL
½ cup	white wine	120 mL
1 cup	lemon juice, fresh	240 mL
	salt and white pepper to taste	
½ cup	pearl onions, whole	120 mL

Cut the peppers, carrot, zucchinis, and celery stalk into narrow strips, then cut on an angle to form diamond-shape pieces.

In cold water, wash, scrub, and remove the beards from the mussels. Discard any broken or open mussels. In a large frying pan on high heat, toss in the mussels, shallots, white wine, and lemon juice. Cover and steam for 3 minutes. Remove the mussels from the pot and set the broth aside for later. Carefully remove half of each mussel shell, keeping only the shell that contains the meat of the mussel.

Pour the mussel broth through a fine strainer and stir into the warm White Wine and Lemon Butter Sauce. Toss the mussels into this mixture and add the finely cut vegetables. Continue stirring for about 3 minutes, or until the vegetables are tender. Season to taste and keep warm until ready to serve.

Part 3: The Arctic Char

4	6-oz. (170-g) Arctic Char fillets	4
	salt and white pepper to taste	
1 Tbsp.	paprika	15 mL
¼ cup	flour	60 mL
¼ cup	olive oil	60 mL
1 Tbsp.	unsalted butter	15 mL

Preheat the oven to 400°F (200°C). Season the fish with salt and pepper. Combine the paprika and flour and dredge the fish portions. Pat off the excess flour. In a hot, ovenproof skillet, heat oil and butter. Place flesh-side down in the hot pan and cook for 2 minutes. Turn the fish to the skin side, and bake in the oven for 8–10 minutes or until it has an internal temperature of 130°F (54°C).

Reduce the oven to 350°F (175°C). Carefully remove the skin from the fish. Place these skins on a baking sheet and bake for 5 minutes until they are dry and become firm and crispy. Remove and place onto a paper towel.

Presentation: Quickly place the fish onto warmed plates and press the crispy skin into the fish flesh, to act as a "sail" for your "windsurfer." Drizzle the Mussel Citrus Stew around the fish.

Roasted Cod on Zucchini Relish

Serves 4

Cod isn't just for children's fish fingers anymore. It is a mild, flaky fish that is inexpensive and light.

Part 1: Curry-Scented Zucchini Relish

½ cup	olive oil	120 mL
1	small green zucchini, finely diced	1
1	small yellow zucchini, finely diced	1
1	small onion, finely diced	1
1	clove garlic, minced	1
2 Tbsp.	sugar	30 mL
2 Tbsp.	curry powder	30 mL
¼ cup	cider vinegar	60 mL
1 Tbsp.	mustard seed	15 mL
	salt and black pepper to taste	

In a large frying pan, heat half the olive oil and quickly sauté the zucchini until tender. Place in a bowl. With the remaining oil, sweat off the onion, garlic, sugar, curry powder, and cider vinegar. Reduce by 80%. Fold in the mustard seeds. Add the onion and curry mixture to the zucchini in the bowl. Mix together and strain off any excess oil. Add seasonings.

Part 2: The Roasted Cod

4	6-oz. (170-g) cod portions, skin on	4
	salt and pepper to taste	
1 Tbsp.	paprika	15 mL
½ cup	flour	120 mL
½ cup	olive oil	120 mL
2 Tbsp.	unsalted butter	30 mL

Preheat the oven to 400°F (200°C). Season the fish portions with salt and pepper. Combine the paprika and flour and dredge the fish. Pat off excess flour. In an ovenproof frying pan, heat the olive oil and butter and place the fish skin-side down and sear for two minutes. Put the pan in the oven and bake for 5 minutes until the fish is flaky. Remove from the pan and pat off any excess oil or butter.

Presentation: Place the fish in the center of warmed plates, add a couple of spoonfuls of relish, half on and half off the fish.

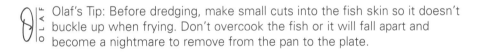

Olaf's Tip: Before dredging, make small cuts into the fish skin so it doesn't buckle up when frying. Don't overcook the fish or it will fall apart and become a nightmare to remove from the pan to the plate.

Shrimp in Love

Serves 4

For a perfect romantic dinner, all you really need are Shrimp in Love, a loaf of crusty bread, your favorite wine—and a date! Although this makes an excellent appetizer, it is also great when served with rice or pasta as a main course. It's the best way to eat shrimp.

20	jumbo tiger shrimp, deveined, cleaned, and butterflied	20
2 Tbsp.	olive oil	30 mL
2	cloves garlic, minced	2
1 Tbsp.	minced shallots or 1 small onion, minced	15 mL
½ cup	brandy	120 mL
1 cup	tomato sauce	240 mL
1 cup	35% cream	240 mL
	salt and white pepper to taste	
½ cup	finely sliced green onions or scallions	120 mL
1 Tbsp.	cold unsalted butter, cubed	15 mL

In a large frying pan on medium heat, sauté the shrimp quickly (about 2 minutes) in the olive oil to medium-rare and remove from the pan. Using the flavors already in the pan, sweat the garlic and shallots to a light brown. Deglaze with the brandy, then add the tomato sauce and cream. Simmer 3 minutes, and add seasonings. Return the shrimp to the pan. Add the green onions or scallions and whisk in the cold butter cubes.

Presentation: Piggyback the 5 shrimp upon each other on each of the plates and cover with the sauce. That's why they are in love!

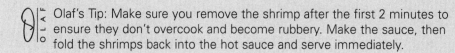 Olaf's Tip: Make sure you remove the shrimp after the first 2 minutes to ensure they don't overcook and become rubbery. Make the sauce, then fold the shrimps back into the hot sauce and serve immediately.

Steamed Mussels in Sabayon

Serves 4

This is a fantastic appetizer or a small meal for the mussel lover. My sous-chef, Ryan Skelton, created this dish for me. Some things are just made to share with others. You can use a drier white wine than a Riesling, but the sweetness of this wine really makes the flavor unique.

2 lbs.	fresh Prince Edward Island or other cultivated mussels	900 g
1	clove garlic, minced	1
1	shallot, minced	1
	salt and white pepper to taste	
½ cup	Riesling wine (or other dry white wine)	120 mL
1 tsp.	Dijon mustard	5 mL
1	large egg	1
	salt to taste	
1 cup	Riesling wine (or other dry white wine)	240 mL
1 tsp.	hot pepper sauce	5 mL
1 Tbsp.	cracked peppercorns	15 mL
2 Tbsp.	steamed mussel liquid	30 mL
12	large basil leaves	12
1 tsp.	lemon juice	5 mL

In cold water, wash, scrub, and remove the beards from the mussels. Discard any that are broken or open. In a large pot, sauté the mussels, garlic, and shallot seasoned with a little salt and white pepper to taste. Add the ½ cup (120 mL) of wine and cover. Steam just until mussels open. When cooked, strain the mussels through a fine mesh strainer, but save this liquid.

To make the sabayon, combine the mustard, egg, and salt in a stainless steel bowl. Whisk until smooth and light. Add the 1 cup (240 mL) of wine, hot pepper sauce, pepper, and the strained mussel liquid. Cook while whisking constantly over a pot of gently simmering water. Once this mixture is thick and foamy, remove from heat.

Presentation: Arrange the mussels on a platter or plates and drizzle with the sabayon. To garnish, stack the basil leaves, then roll together to make one roll. Slice into fine slices or strips. (You can now "chiffonade" basil!) Toss with lemon juice and sprinkle over the plated mussels.

Olaf's Tip: Fresh mussels are a must! Make sure all the mussels are fully open. Discard any that do not open during steaming. Cook with the mussel liquid to get wonderful flavors.

The Main Course

My other true love—when it comes to the kitchen—is that of "saucier"—the position in the kitchen that specializes in preparing meats and fish and presenting them in an enormous range of sauces. This would prove to be my forte; I have probably spent at least half of my culinary life cooking meat, fish, and sauces.

Prime cuts are great to cook, especially when you learn some tricks of the trade for bringing out the natural flavors. But to me the real challenge is to cook secondary cuts. These are the cheaper cuts of meat that, with time and nurturing, result in delicious, tender dishes, often with spectacular sauces.

When we think of the German cuisine, meat and potatoes come to mind. Certainly, in Germany, the saucier in a large hotel kitchen is the workhorse of the whole environment. When I was learning to be a saucier, my teachers seemed to teach everything the hard way. But they were the technically superior ways, and I guess that's why I remembered these approaches the most. As with any skill, true expertise is in the little details. And those details are what turns the ordinary into the extraordinary!

In this collection of recipes, I have taken some classic recipes that I learned in school and jazzed them up. I've twisted them by choosing different ingredients and lively combinations to make them exciting. Some of the recipes are easy enough to make for your family for dinner tonight, like my Schnitzel Stacks or Grilled Smoked Pork Chops. Others you might want to save for special occasions—those times when you want to challenge yourself and really knock your guests' socks off!

Serves 4

Once, after I'd had a long flight to Europe, my Oma had this dish ready and waiting for me. I'll never forget what a wonderful welcome that was. If you ever find yourself dining at my Oma's, don't leave anything on your plate or else! Serve this dish with Lemon Caper Relish, page 158, and Potato Brats, page 149.

8	3-oz. (85-g) veal scallopini	8
	salt and pepper to taste	
½ cup	flour	120 mL
½ cup	35% cream	120 mL
2	large eggs	2
½ cup	35% cream, whipped	120 mL
3–4 cups	dry bread crumbs	720–960 mL
½ cup	unsalted butter	120 mL
	vegetable oil for frying	

Season the veal cutlets with salt and pepper. Take three flat bowls. In the first bowl, put the flour. In the second bowl, whisk the liquid cream with the eggs and fold in the whipped cream. In the third bowl put the bread crumbs. Dredge each piece of veal in the flour, pat off any excess, and dip into the cream mixture. Press into the bread crumbs on both sides. Chill the breaded meat for 30 minutes. Heat a deep frying pan with the butter and oil to medium-high and pan-fry the cutlets until golden brown. Remove onto a paper towel and pat off any excess cooking oil.

Presentation: To present this dish, stack two pieces of veal, one on top of each other, to one side of each plate and top with a large spoonful of Lemon Caper Relish. Put the Potato Brats on the other side of the plate.

 Olaf's Tip: By using whipped cream along with the regular cream, you will get a much crispier coating. You could substitute the veal with pork or chicken.

Barbecue Stuffed Veal Chops
with Sun-Dried Tomatoes, Arugula, Basil, and Asiago Cheese

Serves 4

This is a big boys' barbecue meal. By now you know I can't just grill a plain veal chop; I have to alter it slightly. It's in my nature—just ask my wife!

4	12-oz. (340-g) rib-eye veal chops, bone in	4
2 Tbsp.	vegetable oil	30 mL
1	small onion, finely sliced	1
3	cloves garlic, finely sliced	3
2 cups	arugula greens	480 mL
1 cup	sun-dried tomatoes, soaked in hot water	240 mL
1 cup	coarsely chopped fresh basil leaves	240 mL
	salt and pepper to taste	
1 cup	grated Asiago cheese	240 mL
½ cup	fresh white bread crumbs*	120 mL
½ cup	olive oil	120 mL
1	lemon, juice and fine zest of	1
	kosher salt and cracked black peppercorns to taste	
	*See Glossary, page 202.	

With each veal chop, make a 2-inch (5-cm) slice from the bottom of the chop by the bone to the center of the chop. Using your finger, work a center pocket in the middle of the chop.

In a large frying pan, heat the oil and roast the onion and garlic slices until golden brown and tender. Add the arugula greens, tomatoes, and basil. Toss this mixture in a large bowl and add the cheese, bread crumbs, salt, and pepper. Stuff each of the veal chops with ½ cup (120 mL) of the filling.

Preheat the barbecue to 450°F (230°C). In a small bowl, whisk the olive oil, lemon juice, fine zest, kosher salt, and cracked black pepper. Grill the chops for 8 minutes on each side or until the meat reaches an internal temperature of 130°F (54°C). Baste with the lemon juice mixture. Let rest for 10 minutes before serving.

This meal could be completed with grilled vegetables and a potato dish of your choice.

Olaf's Tip: Make sure the pocket is stuffed tightly so that the meat cooks evenly from the inside. You could substitute this veal chop with a beef rib chop or a double pork chop. I love to use kosher salt, especially in this type of recipe, since it packs a little flavor punch and texture.

Surf and Turf Wellington
with Basil Cream Sauce and Lemon Butter Sauce

Serves 4

A delicious and unique dish, perfect for a dinner party. It's quite a bit of work, but you can prepare it ahead of time, then just bake and serve when your guests arrive. Traditional Beef Wellington is beef fillet with mushrooms and foie gras wrapped in puff pastry, but as you have seen, I love to twist the classics to make them new, fresh, and fun. I don't want to scare you off, but this recipe is for those who are looking for a challenge.

4 Tbsp.	olive oil	60 mL
1 lb.	veal tenderloin	455 g
	salt and pepper to taste	
6	large portobello mushrooms caps	6
1 lb.	Atlantic salmon, cut into long, tubular chunks	455 g
1	bundle bok choy, leaves only	1
2	large semi-ripe mangos, peeled	2
1 lb.	puff pastry, store-purchased, thawed	455 g
3 cups	ground chicken	720 mL
1 cup	whipping cream	240 mL
½ cup	sliced fresh chives	120 mL
	salt and white pepper to taste	
1	large egg yolk	1
¼ cup	whole milk	60 mL
1 recipe	White Wine and Lemon Butter Sauce (page 26)	1 recipe
1 recipe	Basil Cream Sauce (page 27)	1 recipe

In a large pan, heat half the oil to high. Season the veal tenderloin with salt and pepper and sear in the hot oil, rolling to brown all sides. Set aside. Using the hot oil in this pan, quickly sauté the mushrooms until wilted. Remove to paper towels to dry off excess oil, and set aside.

In another pan, add the remaining oil, sear all sides of the salmon and remove to paper towels to dry off excess oil. Set these aside also.

In a pot of boiling salted water, quickly drop in the cleaned bok choy. Remove after 30 seconds. Quickly place in an ice-cold water bath, then remove from the water, open the leaves, and dry them on a cloth.

Cut the mushroom caps in half horizontally diagonally to make two large circles from each mushroom cap. Slice the peeled mango into large slices.

Roll out half the puff pastry to ¼-inch (.6-cm) thickness and approximately 12 x 16 inches (30-cm x 40-cm) and chill. Repeat with the second half of the pastry and put aside to make a lid.

In a small bowl, mix the ground chicken, whipping cream, chives, and seasonings.

On a piece of plastic wrap about 16 inches (40 cm) long, place the mushroom slices down just overlapping each other to make approximately an 8- x 12-inch (20-cm x 30-cm) rectangle. Top with about ½ cup (120 mL) of the ground chicken mixture, leaving 2½ cups (600 mL) of the mixture to use later. Place the veal down the length of the mushroom and chicken mixture. Using the plastic wrap for leverage, roll the mixture around the veal as tightly as possible. Be careful not to let the plastic wrap get caught in the roll. Seal the ends of the plastic wrap around the roll and refrigerate until ready to assemble.

On another piece of plastic wrap about 16 inches (40 cm) long, place the mango slices to make an 8- x 12-inch (20-cm x 30-cm) rectangle. Spread ½ cup (120 mL) of the ground chicken mixture on top of the mango slices, then cover with bok choy, then another ½ cup (120 mL) of the chicken mixture, and place the seared salmon on top. You should still have about 1½ cups (360 mL) of the chicken mixture left. As with the veal, roll as tightly as you can, seal the ends of the wrap, and refrigerate until ready to assemble.

continued on next page

Preheat the oven to 450°F (230°C). On a parchment-lined baking sheet, take one of the chilled puff pastry rectangles and on it, spread a ½-inch (1.2-cm) layer of the chicken mixture right up to about 1 inch (2.5 cm) from the edges. Unwrap the veal tenderloin roll and the salmon roll and place them side by side lengthwise on the pastry. Using the remaining chicken mixture, fill the gap between the two rolls. Wash the edges of the bottom pastry rectangle with an egg wash made with the egg yolk and milk. Take the second puff pastry rectangle and, as tightly as possible, place it over the two rolls. Press all around the edges to seal the pastry. Egg-wash the entire surface to get a nice sheen when baked. Bake for 10 minutes to brown the pastry and then lower the heat to 350°F (175°C) for 25 minutes to allow the veal and salmon to cook. This should give you a medium-rare center and an internal temperature of 130°F (54°C). Let the parcel rest for 10 minutes before slicing.

While this is baking, prepare the White Wine and Lemon Butter Sauce and the Basil Cream Sauce. Place a pool of the Basil Cream Sauce on one side of the plate and the White Wine and Lemon Butter Sauce on the other. Place a slice of veal wellington on the basil cream sauce and the salmon wellington on the lemon butter sauce.

Olaf's Tip: The entire dish can be made up to one day before you want to serve it. Plan to make it well beforehand so that you are less stressed when your guests arrive.

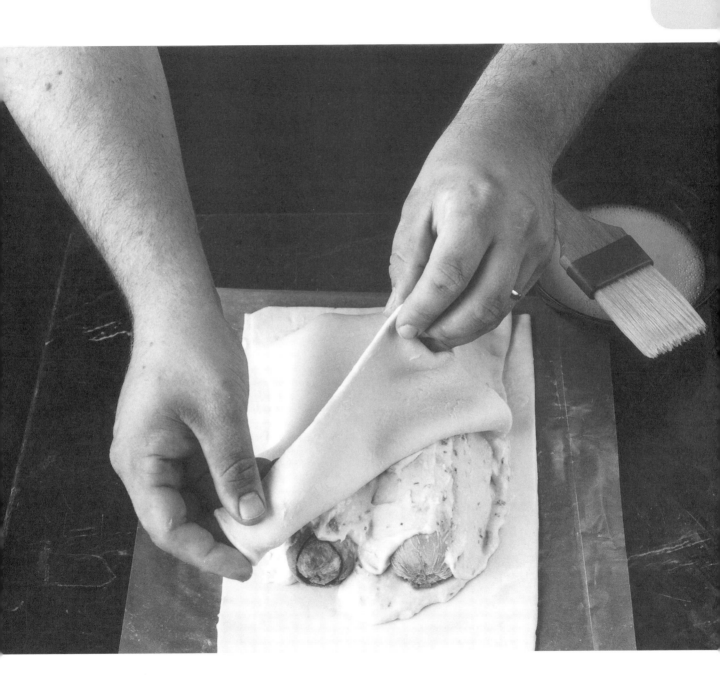

Roast Pork Rack Chops
with Maple and Dark Beer Sauce

Serves 4

Roast pork and beer—what a partnership! Serving a roast at a dinner party is an excellent choice, as it fills your kitchen with wonderful smells and gives you time with your guests, or time to serve a course or two prior to the main course. This glaze is a very rich sauce, so only a small amount is needed.

Part 1: Maple and Dark Beer Sauce

¼ cup	vegetable oil	60 mL
4	cloves garlic, sliced	4
1 cup	diced shallots	240 mL
1	12-oz. (340-mL) bottle dark beer	1
1 cup	balsamic vinegar	240 mL
¾ cup	maple syrup	180 mL
1 Tbsp.	chopped fresh rosemary	15 mL
1 Tbsp.	chopped fresh thyme	15 mL
1 Tbsp.	Dijon mustard	15 mL
	salt to taste	

In a medium pot on medium heat, heat the oil and slow-roast the garlic and shallots until golden brown. Add the beer, vinegar, and maple syrup and simmer for about 15–20 minutes until it reaches a syrupy consistency. Remove from the heat and add the herbs. Stir in the mustard and add salt to taste. Set aside in a warm place.

Part 2: Pork Rack Chops

4 lbs.	small pork rack, French-chopped, chine bone removed (see Tip)	1.8 kg
	salt and cracked peppercorns	
1 cup	minced garlic	240 mL
4	sprigs fresh thyme, chopped	4
1 cup	mustard powder	240 mL
1 cup	vegetable oil	240 mL
4	sprigs rosemary leaves, chopped	4
¼ cup	minced shallots	60 mL

Preheat the oven to 350°F (175°C). Place the pork rack on a cutting board and cross-hatch the outside layer of fat with a sharp knife. Season well with salt and pepper. Mix the remaining ingredients and rub the mixture into all the surfaces of the pork rack. Bake 1¼ hours or until the meat thermometer reads 140°F (62°C). Let the meat rest in a warm area of the kitchen for at least 20 minutes before carving. Using the bones as a guide, cut the rack into individual chops.

Presentation: Ladle the sauce onto the bottom of the warmed plates, then place individual chops like fallen dominoes on the center of the plates. Accompany with side dishes like Soft Savory Pretzel Bread Dumplings, page 147, and Spicy Braised Plums and Cabbage, page 151.

 Olaf's Tip: "French-chopped rack of pork, chine bone removed" means you have a pork loin roast with only clean, short chop bones (any trace of meat removed) making it easy to slice between the chop bones. Any butcher, with a little notice, can prepare this for you.

Grilled Smoked Pork Chops
with Malt Beer Jus

Serves 4

This dish has a multitude of different flavors. It's an updated version of an Oktoberfest meal that is great any month of the year! Smoked pork loin chops are available at your grocery, as well as any European deli. The malt beer makes a fantastic sauce, and beer and pork are a super combination. Just make sure that the beer is not too bitter. And be sure to have enough to sip on while you're cooking.

Part 1: Malt Beer Jus

½ cup	vegetable oil	120 mL
1	small onion, sliced	1
1	sprig rosemary leaves, chopped	1
½ cup	sugar	120 mL
1	12-oz. (340-mL) bottle dark malt beer	1
¼ cup	molasses	60 mL
⅓ cup	honey	80 mL
¼ cup	cider vinegar	60 mL
½ cup	Dijon mustard	120 mL
¼ cup	cold unsalted butter, cubed	60 mL
	salt and black pepper to taste	

In a medium-sized, heavy-bottomed pot, heat the oil over medium heat. Sauté the onions and rosemary until the onions are translucent. Add the sugar and let caramelize to a dark caramel color. Watch carefully and stir constantly, as this is easy to burn! Deglaze with the beer, being careful of rising steam. The sugar will harden and then melt. Add the molasses, honey, and vinegar, and continue simmering for about 10–15 minutes or until the mixture is reduced by ¾. Reduce heat to minimum temperature and whisk in the mustard and cold butter. Season to taste. Keep warm.

Part 2: Smoked Pork Chops

4   8-oz. (225-g) smoked pork loin chops 4

Preheat the barbecue to 450°F (230°C). Grill the chops 4 minutes per side or until their internal temperature reaches 140°F (62°C).

Presentation: This is a great "feast"-type food, so you could serve it on big platters instead of individual plates. Drizzle the jus lightly over the top of the meat and put the remainder in gravy boats for guests to serve themselves. I really like this with Warm Potato Salad, page 160, and Pineapple Sauerkraut, page 159.

Olaf's Tip: To give meats the charred checkered pattern that restaurants usually use, turn the direction of the meat 90° when halfway through grilling each side.

Stuffed Chicken Supreme
with Bacon, Roasted Onion, and Cambozola Cheese in Sweet Red Pepper Juices

Serves 4

I love serving stuffed meats—it's the ultimate edible surprise. This is a very tasty and unique filling. It's a best seller at our restaurant. The chicken breasts and the sauce can be prepared a couple of hours ahead and then finished just before serving, so this makes it an excellent choice for entertaining.

Part 1: The Stuffing

¼ cup	vegetable oil	60 mL
1	small onion, thinly sliced	1
½ cup	diced bacon	120 mL
1 cup	crumbled Cambozola cheese, rind removed	240 mL
1	large egg	1
¼ cup	chopped fresh parsley	60 mL
½ cup	dry bread crumbs	120 mL
	salt and white pepper to taste	

In a small pan on medium heat, heat the oil and sauté the onion until golden. Add the diced bacon and cook until crispy. Drain off the excess fat. Place the cheese, egg and parsley in a bowl and quickly mix in the bacon and onion mixture while still warm. Add the bread crumbs and season. This mixture should be tacky to touch but not too wet. If wet, add more bread crumbs. Chill while you prepare the chicken breast.

Part 2: Preparing the Chicken

4	6-oz. (170-g) chicken breasts, skin on	4
4	slices of side bacon	4

On a cutting board covered with plastic wrap, place the breast, skin-side down, with the tenderloin (the finger-like piece of flesh attached to the breast) flipped to one side. Using a sharp knife, make a lengthwise cut down the middle of the breast and about halfway into the thickness of the breast. Inside that cut, make another cut to the left and right of that slit making a pocket on the top of the breast. (See pictures below and page 133.)

Preheat the oven to 350°F (175°C). Place a quarter of the stuffing into each prepared chicken breast pocket. Close the pocket by folding in the sides of the pocket and taking the tenderloin back over to the middle.

Secure by wrapping each breast with a bacon strip. Bake for 20–30 minutes. Allow to rest for 10 minutes before cutting, to keep the juices inside.

continued on next page

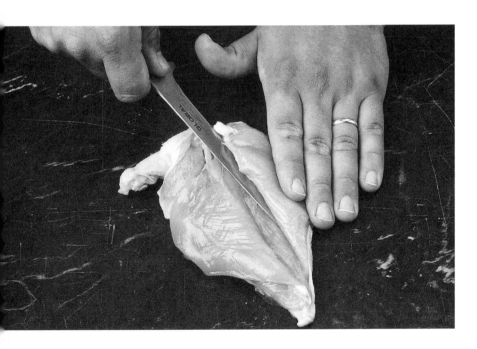

Olaf's Tip: The resting time is very important, not only to have juicy chicken breasts, but also to let the cheese turn solid again, allowing you to cut cleanly. You can substitute the cheese suggested with a cheese of your choice: Brie, cheddar, or goat's cheese.

Part 3: Sweet Red Pepper Juices

2 Tbsp.	vegetable oil	30 mL
1	small onion, diced	1
2	sweet red peppers, diced	2
2 cups	white wine	480 mL
2 cups	Chicken Stock (page 21), or store-purchased	480 mL
3 Tbsp.	ketchup	45 mL
2 Tbsp.	honey	30 mL
	salt and white pepper to taste	
½ cup	cold unsalted butter, cubed	120 mL
⅛ tsp.	lemon juice	.5 mL
	chopped red peppers or parsley for garnish	

In a small pot on medium heat, heat the oil and roast the onion and peppers. Deglaze with the white wine, simmer and reduce 80%. Add the stock and ketchup. Simmer 10 minutes. Add the honey and seasonings. Place the mixture into a food processor or blender and purée. Strain through a mesh strainer into a clean pot. Just before serving, bring the sauce to a simmer and whisk in the cold cubes of butter and lemon juice. Taste and adjust the seasoning if necessary.

Presentation: I serve this dish on a bed of mashed potatoes and freshly prepared vegetables. Divide the sauce equally among the warmed serving plates, place the potatoes in a mound in the center, cut the chicken breast in half to show off the cheese mixture and place on top, and add your choice of vegetables to the side. Sprinkle with some chopped peppers or parsley.

Roast Chicken Breast Supreme
with Shrimp Stuffing and Lemon Sauce

Serves 4

Shrimp birds! To hide the shrimp-like pearls in a "shell" of chicken is a terrific twist. Although stuffing the chicken might be a little complicated, you will perfect it with a little practice. This dish looks fantastic on the plate and tastes amazing.

Part 1: Stuffing the Chicken Breasts

4	6-oz. (170-g) chicken breasts, boneless, skin on	4
¼ cup	unsalted butter	60 mL
1	clove garlic, minced	1
1	small bunch spinach, stems removed	1
1 cup	chopped fresh basil leaves	240 mL
2	sprigs fresh thyme, chopped	2
16	jumbo shrimp	16
	salt and cracked black peppercorns to taste	

On a cutting board covered with plastic wrap, place the breast, skin-side down, with the tenderloin (the finger-like piece of flesh attached to the breast) flipped to one side. Using a sharp knife, make a lengthwise cut down the middle of the breast and about halfway into the thickness of the breast. Inside that cut, make another cut to the left and right of that slit making a pocket on the top of the breast. (See pictures, page 131 and 133.)

In a medium-size pan, over medium heat, melt the butter and sweat off the garlic, spinach, basil, and thyme leaves for about 2 minutes. Remove from the heat. Take the individual cooked spinach leaves from the pot, pat dry with a paper towel. Carefully line the pockets with the spinach leaves. Set a few leaves aside to finish covering the top after filling with shrimp.

Preheat the oven to 350°F (175°C). Toss the shrimp into the pan with the remaining butter and herbs. Sauté for 2 minutes. Push the shrimp into the spinach-lined pockets, being careful not to overfill or you won't be able to close them. Cover the shrimp with the remaining spinach leaves. The shrimp should be completely covered in spinach and chicken as you close the chicken around the stuffing and place the tenderloin back into place as the cover for the hole you stuffed. (At this point the stuffed chicken breast can be sealed tightly and refrigerated up to 24 hours and then baked for 25 minutes before serving.)

Season the chicken breasts with salt and pepper. Bake, skin-side up, for 20 minutes, then crisp up the skin for 3 minutes under a hot broiler to finish.

Allow the chicken breasts to rest for 5 minutes before cutting into 1-inch (2.5-cm) slices crosswise so that you see the shrimp and spinach stuffing surrounded by chicken.

Part 2: Lemon Sauce

1	lemon, juice and zest of	1
1 cup	white wine	240 mL
1 cup	Chicken Stock (page 21), or store-purchased	240 mL
½ cup	cold unsalted butter, cubed	120 mL
	salt and white pepper to taste	

In the roasting pan used to cook the chicken, add the lemon juice, zest, and white wine. Simmer on medium heat and stir. Scrape off the pan roastings. Strain through a mesh strainer into a small pot on medium heat and continue to simmer until reduced by 50%. Then add the stock. Reduce again by 50%. Just before serving, whisk in the cold butter cubes, which will thicken the mixture slightly. Add the seasonings.

Presentation: I garnish this dish with a vegetable medley of white and green asparagus, diced carrots, zucchini, broccoli, red peppers, and Enoki mushrooms. Any or all of these would finish off your dish beautifully. I've also set aside one grilled shrimp per plate as a garnish, but that's strictly optional.

 Olaf's Tip: The stuffing should be as dry as possible. Be especially careful to strain and paper-towel-dry the spinach and the shrimp, since both will naturally have retained a lot of water.

Grilled Lemon Paillard of Turkey

Serves 4

A great meal for an autumn day. Get those outdoor chores done and come in to this amazing treat. You could also serve this dish as a change to the classic Christmas or Thanksgiving turkey. "Paillard" means pieces. I suggest you use the Lemon Caper Relish, page 158, as a great accompaniment to this dish.

Part 1: Vegetable Mix

1	parsnip	1
1	celery bulb	1
1	sweet potato	1
1	large carrot	1
1	large red beet	1
1	cinnamon stick	1
¼ tsp.	cinnamon	1.2 mL
1	vanilla bean, split and scraped	1
½ cup	maple syrup	120 mL
	salt and black pepper to taste	
¼ cup	vegetable oil	60 mL

Preheat the oven to 350°F (175°C). Peel and dice all the vegetables into 1-inch (2.5-cm) pieces. Place all the vegetables in a large bowl. In a small bowl, combine the cinnamon, vanilla bean marrow, maple syrup, salt, pepper, and oil. Pour this mixture over the vegetables until well coated. Place on a non-stick roasting pan or a regular baking sheet lined with parchment paper and bake for 30–35 minutes. Set aside and keep warm.

Part 2: The Turkey

8	4-oz. (113-g) boneless, skinless turkey breasts scallopini	8
1	clove garlic, minced	1
1	lemon, juice and zest of	1
¼ cup	chopped fresh oregano	60 mL
¼ cup	chopped fresh parsley	60 mL
¼ cup	chopped fresh basil	60 mL
1 cup	olive oil	240 mL
	salt and pepper to taste	

With a mallet, pound the turkey breasts to ¼-inch (.6-cm) thickness and place in a shallow baking dish. In a small bowl, mix the remaining ingredients and pour over the turkey breasts. Allow to marinate for 30 minutes. Preheat the barbecue to 450°F (230°C). Grill the turkey slices over a hot grill for 2 minutes on each side.

Presentation: On warmed serving plates, mound the vegetable mix in the center, lay on the turkey slices and top with the Lemon Caper Relish.

 Olaf's Tip: The turkey breast sizes are only approximate. You can purchase enough whole boneless turkey breasts and cut them to the above suggested weights. Barbecue the turkey just before serving your guests. Don't chance drying out the slices.

Roast Duckling
with Red Grapefruit and Green Peppercorn Sauce

Serves 4

This dish is a lot of work, but is oooohhh so worth it. Traditionally, duck is served with an orange glaze or sauce, but once you've tried this sauce, with the tangy sweetness of the ruby red grapefruit, you'll see why this has become a tradition of mine. The duck legs, glaze, and garnish can be prepared a day ahead and reheated while the duck breasts cook.

Part 1: Divide the Ducks!

2	duckings, whole	2
	kosher salt and white pepper	

Detach both legs (thigh attached) from the duck. Carefully remove and debone the breast meat, with the skin intact, from the carcass. This is a bit tricky, so you may want to consider special-ordering this from your butcher. Save the bones. Chill this breast meat while you prepare the legs.

Part 2: Duck Legs

4	duckling quarters (legs and thighs, as prepared above) and duck bones	4
⅓ cup	vegetable oil	80 mL
½ cup	unsalted butter	120 mL
1	carrot, diced	1
2	stalks celery, diced	2
1	onion, diced	1
2	parsnips, diced	2
3 cups	red wine	720 mL
2 cups	Chicken Stock (page 21), or store-purchased	480 mL
2	bay leaves	2
1	sprig fresh rosemary, chopped	1
1	sprig fresh thyme, chopped	1
2	oranges, juice of	2
1	lemon, juice of	1
	salt and white pepper to taste	

Preheat the oven to 350°C (175°C). Using a sharp knife, score the duck skin in a checkerboard pattern. You will need a large, deep oven pan with a removable rack. Remove the rack and place the pan on a high heat and sear the duck legs in the oil. Remove the duck legs from the pan. Add the butter and sauté the vegetables in the same roasting pan. Deglaze with the wine and simmer for 10 minutes. Add the chicken stock, bay leaves, herbs, and citrus juices.

Place the rack on top of the vegetables and put the legs on the rack. Season well with salt and pepper. Cover the pan with tin foil and bake for 30 minutes. Remove the foil and continue cooking for 15–20 minutes or until golden brown. With a fine sieve, strain the pan juices, removing all vegetables and impurities from the juices. Place the legs back into the juices to store until ready to serve. They can be kept 1–2 days like this in the refrigerator.

Part 3: Duck Breasts

Preheat the oven to 350°F (175°C). With a sharp knife, score the skin of the duck breasts through the fatty layer with a fine checkerboard pattern and season well with salt and pepper. Preheat an ovenproof frying pan on high and sear the breasts for 3 minutes per side. Place the duck breast, skin-side down, on a rack in a baking pan and bake in the oven for 15 minutes for medium-rare, or until it reaches an internal temperature of 130°C (54°C). Let rest for 10 minutes before cutting into ¼-inch (.6-cm) slices.

Part 4: Caramelized Red Grapefruit and Green Peppercorn Sauce

½ cup	sugar	120 mL
1 cup	honey	240 mL
¼ cup	red wine vinegar	60 mL
2	ruby red grapefruits, juice of	2
1 Tbsp.	grenadine	15 mL
2 Tbsp.	green peppercorns	30 mL
2 tsp.	peppercorn brine	10 mL

In a medium saucepan over medium heat, slowly cook the sugar for about 3 minutes until it caramelizes. Pour in the honey, vinegar, grapefruit juice, and the grenadine. Simmer for 10–15 minutes. Add the green peppercorns and the brine. Simmer for 15 minutes until thick enough to coat the back of a spoon.

Part 5: Garnish

1	large orange, juice and zests of	1
¼ cup	honey	60 mL
¼ cup	sugar	60 mL
2	ruby red grapefruits, peeled, segments	2

Carefully peel the orange with a vegetable peeler or use a zester, being careful not to leave any of the bitter-tasting white pith. Slice the peels into sliver-thin strips.

In a small pot over medium heat, wilt the orange zest by cooking for about 3–5 minutes in the orange juice and honey until tender. Remove the zests from the juice and dust them in the sugar while still warm. Spread out on a sheet of waxed paper to dry.

Presentation: Place a whole leg on one side of the plates, fan the sliced breast meat beside the legs, and drizzle the glaze around the outside of the plate. Garnish with the grapefruit segments and orange zests. I like to serve this duck with my Potato Finger Noodles, page 32, and a simple green vegetable like broccoli.

 Olaf's Tip: The duck legs, sauce, and garnish can all be prepared up to a day in advance. About 45 minutes before serving, preheat the oven to 350°F (175°C) to reheat the legs for 15–20 minutes. At this time you would continue preparing the duck breasts while slowly heating the sauce on the stove top.

Manny's Colossus Lamb Parcels

Serves 4 to 6

This one is a tribute to my first food critic. I've known him since we were 14 years old: Manny "Lucky" Tsouvallas, a restaurateur with heart, soul, and passion. He taught me how to make this dish, and I took the liberty of turning it into something with a little twist. All the food groups are covered so you can serve it as a meal or course on its own. Lamb parcels—it's just like a Greek birthday!

Part 1: Lamb Loins

1 lb.	lamb loins	455 g
	salt and black pepper to taste	
¼ cup	olive oil	60 mL

Preheat the oven to 350°F (175°C). Season the loins with salt and pepper. In an ovenproof frying pan, heat the oil on medium-high and sear all sides of the loins. Bake in the oven for 5–7 minutes or until the internal temperature reaches 130°F (54°C). Remove from the pan and allow to rest for 10 minutes. Carve into thin, ¼-inch (.6-cm) slices.

Part 2: Lamb and Herb Mixture

1	roasted red pepper*, strips	1
1	roasted yellow pepper*, strips	1
½ cup	Kalamata olives, pitted	120 mL
½ cup	chopped sun-dried tomatoes, soaked in hot water	120 mL
2 cups	crumbled feta cheese	480 mL
1 Tbsp.	chopped fresh thyme	15 mL
16	leaves fresh basil, sliced	16
1 Tbsp.	chopped fresh oregano leaves	15 mL
16	leaves fresh mint, sliced	16
2	cloves roasted garlic, minced	2
½ cup	sliced scallions	120 mL
2 Tbsp.	Dijon mustard	30 mL
	salt and black pepper to taste	

*See page 43 for directions on roasting peppers.

In a large bowl, combine all the above ingredients with the lamb loin slices. Set aside.

Olaf's Tip: You can use oil-packed sun-dried tomatoes; just drain off the oil first.

Part 3: Phyllo Pastry Parcels

1 lb.	package phyllo pastry, store-purchased, thawed	455 g
1 cup	melted butter	240 mL
	chopped oregano, or a sprig of oregano or mint for garnish	

Preheat the oven to 350°F (175°C). Unroll the phyllo pastry and immediately cover with a damp cloth to prevent it from drying out. Place one sheet on a flat surface and brush with melted butter. Repeat until you have three layers of buttered sheets ready. Place a quarter of the lamb mixture in the middle of the narrow side of the pastry, and roll one full roll, fold in the two sides of the pastry, and continue to roll to make a neat tubular parcel. Brush all surfaces with melted butter. Place parcels on a parchment paper-lined baking sheet and bake for 15 minutes.

Presentation: This is simply presented with a large pool of Cherry Tomato Dressing, page 108, served with the lamb parcel in the middle. Garnish with chopped oregano or a sprig of oregano or mint.

Olaf's Tip: This is a great lamb dish, and a great way to use up your leftovers. If you don't have lamb, use beef or pork roast leftovers. It's not as Greek, but it tastes just as good.

Beer-Braised Lamb and Bean Ragout

Serves 4

½ cup	olive oil	120 mL
1¾ lbs.	lamb shoulder, 1-inch (2.5-cm) pieces	800 g
4	large onions, ¼-inch (.6-cm) slices	4
2	cloves garlic, minced	2
	salt and black pepper to taste	
2 Tbsp.	paprika	30 mL
1 Tbsp.	caraway seeds	15 mL
4 Tbsp.	flour	60 mL
1 cup	white navy beans, pre-soaked	240 mL
2	12-oz. (340-mL) bottles beer	2
2 cups	green beans, snipped	480 mL
1 Tbsp.	sugar	15 mL
1 Tbsp.	chopped fresh thyme	15 mL
¼ cup	chopped fresh parsley	60 mL

Heat the olive oil in a large pot over medium-high heat. Sear the lamb pieces to brown all sides. Reduce the heat to medium and add the onions and minced garlic. Sauté until golden brown. Season well and add the paprika, caraway seeds, and flour. Drain the white beans and add to the mixture. Add the beer and slowly simmer for 45–60 minutes until the meat is tender. Add the green beans, sugar, and herbs. Add any salt and pepper to taste. Simmer for an additional 5 minutes.

Presentation: Serve with Potato Brats, page 149, or just place a hearty serving in a soup bowl served with fresh chunks of rye bread. Ragout, beer, and rye bread—let the cold nights come.

 Olaf's Tip: The hops in the beer gives this recipe much added flavor. The sugar is used to balance the bitterness of the beer.

Herb Crusted Beef Fillets
with Horseradish Vegetable Stew

Serves 4

Beef and horseradish—an old classic, lightly crusted with a butter herb topping.

Part 1: Herb Crust (page 33)

Part 2: Horseradish Vegetable Stew

1 recipe	Basil Cream Sauce (page 27)	1 recipe
1	large carrot, thinly sliced circles	1
1	red pepper, strips	1
1 cup	pearl onions, blanched	240 mL
1 cup	sugar snap peas, cleaned	240 mL
2 Tbsp.	prepared horseradish, or to taste	30 mL
2 Tbsp.	chopped fresh chives	30 mL

Prepare the sauce, then add the vegetables. Simmer for 5 minutes until the vegetables are tender. Just before serving, stir in the horseradish and chives. Keep warm.

Part 3: Beef Fillets

4	6-oz. (170-g) beef fillets	4
	salt and black pepper	
2 Tbsp.	vegetable oil	30 mL
2	sprigs rosemary or thyme for garnish	2

Preheat the oven to 375°F (190°C). Heat a large ovenproof frying pan over high heat. Season the beef well. Add the oil to the pan and sear the fillets on all sides. Place in the oven and bake for 8 minutes. Remove from the oven, turn over the fillets, press the herb crust onto that side of the fillets, and return to the oven for another 8 minutes until medium-rare or when the internal temperature reaches 130°F (52°C). Remove from the pan and let rest 5 minutes before serving.

Presentation: Pool the vegetables in their sauce into the middle of warmed serving plates and top with the crusted fillet. Garnish with rosemary or thyme sprigs.

Olaf's Tip: It is very important that you sear all sides of the fillet to ensure that the maximum juices are captured.

Side Dishes

I am fortunate to live in the vicinity of the city of Toronto. This "Golden Horseshoe" area, as it is called, offers fantastic, fresh produce grown locally. The Niagara Peninsula is famous for its fruits and wines. Just north of Toronto is the Holland Marsh where, in its little valley, grow some of the finest vegetables available. There are even some wild patches very near me that, for a very short time, produce exotic mushrooms, leeks, and fiddleheads. Most larger cities these days have access to all the foods the world has to offer—if you can't find what you're looking for, speak to the produce manager at a good grocery store. I know he or she will be able to help you. Even the chefs at fine restaurants may be able to help you find what you need.

My location gives me access to an abundance of fresh ingredients that can ultimately become meals just on their own. But in this chapter, the produce appears in dishes of unique combinations and flavors, with complex textures, that are wonderful companions to a main course.

Serves 4

The British have Yorkshire pudding; Germans have bread dumplings. They are a yummy alternative to potatoes or bread with a meal, designed to sop up tasty gravies. Let me tell you, I've made many bread dumplings in my day, but to make them unique, I use soft pretzels. This is a great accompaniment to the Roast Pork Rack Chops, page 126.

1 lb.	stale soft pretzels, diced	455 g
2 Tbsp.	unsalted butter	30 mL
1 cup	double-smoked bacon*, rind removed, or side bacon, finely diced	240 mL
1	small onion, diced	1
¼ cup	chopped fresh parsley	60 mL
3 cups	whole milk	720 mL
5	egg yolks	5
	salt and black pepper to taste	
¼ cup	unsalted butter, melted	60 mL
	(bread crumbs, if needed)	
	*See Glossary, page 202.	

In a large bowl, break up the pretzels. In a small pan, melt the butter and sauté the bacon and onion until golden brown. Add to the bowl of pretzels along with the chopped parsley and toss. Slowly warm the milk and, while still warm, pour it over the pretzels and then beat in the egg yolks and mix quickly. Season. This mixture should be dry but slightly tacky to touch. If not, add some bread crumbs. Divide the mixture into 4 and, with your hands, make round balls, or dumplings. Let the dumplings rest in the refrigerator until well chilled. Poach in boiling salted water for 3–5 minutes until they float to the surface. Remove, toss in melted butter, and serve.

 Olaf's Tip: Serve these dumplings warm with any meat, but be sure to make lots of gravy. Soft pretzels are available at grocery stores, bakeries, and, of course, baseball stadiums.

Red Nugget Potato, Roasted Cauliflower, and Cheddar Cheese Smash

Serves 4

This is an easy way to please your crowd. This dish is simply mashed potatoes "twisted" into a pretty, colorful, chunky-textured, and tasty concoction. It is easy to make and lets you be ahead of the game—just reheat when you're ready to serve.

4	large, red-skinned mini potatoes	4
1	small cauliflower	1
½ cup	olive oil	120 mL
1 tsp.	salt	5 mL
½ cup	unsalted butter	120 mL
2	cloves garlic, minced	2
1 cup	finely diced scallions	240 mL
¼ tsp.	nutmeg	1.2 mL
1 cup	grated cheddar cheese	240 mL
1½ cups	35% cream	360 mL
	salt and black pepper to taste	

Preheat the oven to 350°F (175°C). Boil the potatoes in salted water until tender and drain well. Break up the cauliflower into 2-inch (5-cm) pieces and toss them in the olive oil and salt. Place on a baking sheet and bake for 15 minutes until tender and golden brown. Mix the two together and smash with a potato masher until it is in chunky, fork-sized pieces.

Meanwhile, in a small pot, melt the butter to a light brown to give it a nutty flavor. Add the garlic and sauté until light brown. Add to the potato and cauliflower mixture. Then add the scallions, nutmeg, cheese, and cream. Mix well. Add the seasonings.

 Olaf's Tip: Scrub the potatoes well so that you can leave the skins on and increase the nutritional value and the color of the dish.

Serves 4

"Brats" is a German word meaning to fry or roast. Crispy, golden-brown roasted potatoes—not just for breakfast, but also a great side dish. Use up your potatoes from yesterday's dinner without them looking like leftovers!

¼ cup	vegetable oil	60 mL
4	medium Yukon Gold potatoes, unpeeled	4
1	large onion, cut into rings	1
¼ lb.	double-smoked bacon*, rind removed, sliced	113 g
1 Tbsp.	unsalted butter	15 mL
	salt and black pepper to taste	
½ cup	sliced fresh chives	120 mL
	*See Glossary, page 202.	

Boil the potatoes with the skins on for about 35 minutes or until fork-tender. Slice the potatoes into ½-inch (1.2-cm) slices, keeping the skin on!

In a large frying pan, heat the oil to medium and roast the potato slices until golden brown. Do not stir. Let them get crispy. Turn the slices over and cover with the onion rings and continue cooking until the onions wilt. Add the bacon and sauté. Finally, add the butter for a nutty flavor. Drain off any excess oil, season, and sprinkle with chives. Serve hot.

Olaf's Tip: Do not stir the potatoes too soon. Let them crisp up first, then carefully turn them over to brown on the other side. This way they won't crumble into pieces.

Vegetable Fricassée

Serves 4

In this dish, the vegetables are roasted quickly until tender but with a bite, and then surrounded in a butter syrup of rich broth—really natural flavors. Serve with roasted fish or chicken breasts.

½ lb.	oyster mushrooms, sliced	225 g
1	small onion, finely diced	1
1 cup	pearl onions, peeled	240 mL
1	large carrot, finely diced	1
½ cup	cold unsalted butter, cubed	120 mL
2 cups	Vegetable Stock (page 23), or store-purchased	480 mL
1 lb.	green asparagus, sliced into ½-inch (1.2-cm) pieces	455 g
2 cups	sweet garden peas	480 mL
¼ cup	chopped fresh parsley	60 mL
¼ cup	chopped fresh chives	60 mL

Heat a large frying pan to medium-high and add the mushrooms, onions, and carrot. Cook until lightly roasted. Add ¼ cup (60 mL) of the butter and 1½ cups (360 mL) of the stock and simmer until the vegetables are tender but slightly crunchy. To finish, pour in the remaining ½ cup (120 mL) stock and stir in the remaining butter. Fold in the asparagus, sweet peas, parsley, and chives. The vegetables should be glazed in a light buttery sauce. Let simmer for 3 minutes and then serve.

Presentation: You can serve this in a soup terrine and have the guests ladle out their own helpings. Or you can place a portion on the side of dinner plates. It's also a nice vegetarian meal when served over rice.

Spicy Braised Plums
and Cabbage

Serves 4

Marinates 24 hours

This is the vegetable that is served when chefs visit chefs. Chef Anna Olson made it for me on a visit to her home. I loved it so much I recreated it the next day for my family. I hope I got it right. A lot of people don't eat green vegetables. Just accept it and make this instead!

½	head red cabbage, shredded	½
1 cup	red currant jam	240 mL
1	cinnamon stick	1
1 cup	red wine	240 mL
1 cup	vegetable oil	240 mL
2	red Bermuda onions, sliced	2
1 tsp.	red chili flakes	5 mL
2 cups	black plums, pitted and sliced	480 mL
4 cups	red wine	960 mL
¼ tsp.	ground cloves	1.2 mL
½ tsp.	sugar	2.5 mL
2 Tbsp.	salt	30 mL
½ tsp.	white pepper	2.5 mL

Toss the cabbage, jam, cinnamon stick, and red wine together and marinate in a glass container, refrigerated, for at least 24 hours.

In a large pot, heat the oil and sweat off the onions until tender. Add the marinated cabbage mixture. Add the remaining ingredients, mix well, and simmer for 60 minutes or until the cabbage is tender and the juices are syrup-like. Serve warm.

 Olaf's Tip: Slowly simmer the mixture and don't overcook it or the cabbage will turn blue! You can easily make this ahead and reheat before serving. If you don't have fresh plums, use canned, but drain off the sweet syrup.

Vegetable Strudel on an Oyster Mushroom Sauce

Serves 4

A warm starter dish: market vegetables rolled in a crisp butter pastry and finished with a chunky oyster mushroom sauce. This strudel can be baked and then stored in the refrigerator or freezer. Imagine coming home late and tired and knowing this dish is there, ready to be warmed up.

Part 1: The Strudel

1 recipe	Strudel Dough (page 36)	1 recipe
½ lb.	green beans, blanched tender	225 g
2 cups	corn, poached off the cob or frozen	480 mL
2 cups	green sugar peas, blanched	480 mL
2	large carrots, sliced and blanched	2
1	head cauliflower, cut in rosettes and blanched	1
1	head broccoli, cut in rosettes and blanched	1
1	medium red onion, thinly sliced	1
1	red pepper, cubed	1
1	yellow pepper, cubed	1
½ cup	sliced fresh chives	120 mL
1 cup	melted unsalted butter	240 mL
	salt and pepper to taste	
1 cup	Parmesan cheese	240 mL
2 cups	fresh white bread crumbs*	480 mL
½ cup	chopped fresh parsley	120 mL
	melted butter for brushing	
	*See Glossary, page 202.	

Place all the prepared vegetables and the chives in a large bowl. Pour the melted butter over, season, and add the cheese, bread crumbs, and parsley. Toss to mix well.

Preheat the oven to 350°F (175°C). To prepare the strudel, see the method in Strudel Dough, page 36. You will end up with about a 3-foot (90-cm) log of strudel. Twist off lengths, like sausage links, that will fit onto your baking tray. Brush the top with melted butter and bake for 20 minutes until golden brown.

Olaf's Tip: Make manageable-sized logs, and then you can twist off rolls that fit onto your baking sheet. This strudel can be baked and then put in the freezer for an emergency dinner. Defrost the strudel and slowly reheat at 225°F (105°C) for 20 minutes. This will warm the center and keep the pastry dry and crisp.

Part 2: Oyster Mushroom Sauce

¼ cup	unsalted butter	60 mL
2 cups	sliced oyster mushrooms	480 mL
1	small white onion, diced	1
1 cup	white wine	240 mL
1 Tbsp.	lemon juice	15 mL
2 cups	35% cream	480 mL
	salt and white pepper to taste	
¼ cup	sliced fresh chives	60 mL

In a small pan, melt the butter and sauté the mushrooms. Remove half of the mushrooms onto a side plate and set aside. Add the onions to the pan with the remaining mushrooms and sweat until the onions are translucent. Deglaze with the white wine and lemon juice and reduce by 80%. Add the cream and simmer for 5 minutes or until it thickens enough to coat the back of a spoon. Add the seasonings. Purée the mixture in a blender and then return to the pan. Add the reserved mushrooms and chives. Serve immediately or simmer on low to heat it up when ready to serve.

Presentation: Cut the strudel into 1½ -inch (3.8-cm) slices and carefully put on a side or dessert plate. Pool the mushroom sauce around the outside. You can also serve sliced on your main course plate and lightly spoon the sauce over one side.

Olaf's Tip: Oyster mushrooms are very fine and delicate and have a light, earthy taste. They are readily available at any grocery store, but can be substituted with a white or brown button mushroom.

"A Study of Parsnips"
Chips on a Vanilla Purée with
Honey Vanilla Roasted Parsnips

Serves 4

Honey vanilla roasted parsnips, parsnip purée, and parsnip chips! It's a lot of "studying," but if you work hard, you will have a great graduation! You will need 16 peeled parsnips altogether for your three different "studies"!

Part 1: Whole Roasted Parsnips

1 cup	brown sugar	240 mL
1	vanilla bean, split and scraped	1
1	cinnamon stick	1
1 cup	honey	240 mL
½ cup	melted unsalted butter	120 mL
1 tsp.	cinnamon	5 mL
2 cups	water	480 mL
8	small parsnips, peeled	8

Preheat the oven to 250° F (120°C). Mix the first seven ingredients together in a large bowl. Toss in the parsnips to coat. Spread out the coated parsnips onto a cookie sheet and slow-roast for 30 minutes, then turn and continue to roast another 20 minutes until tender and golden brown on both sides.

Part 2: Parsnip Purée

½ cup	unsalted butter	120 mL
1	small onion, diced	1
6	parsnips, peeled and diced	6
1 Tbsp.	sugar	15 mL
1 cup	white rice	240 mL
2 cups	Vegetable Stock (page 23), or store-purchased	480 mL
3 cups	35% cream	720 mL
	salt and white pepper to taste	

In a small pot on medium heat, melt the butter and sweat off the onions, parsnips, and sugar for 3 minutes. Add the rice, vegetable stock, and cream and simmer for 30 minutes or until the vegetables and rice are tender and all the liquids have been absorbed. Purée in a food processor, season, and keep warm.

Part 3: Parsnip Crisps

2	large parsnips, peeled and thinly sliced lengthwise	2
	vegetable oil for deep-frying	
	salt and white pepper to taste	

Heat the oil to 310°F (154°C) and quickly deep-fry, a few at a time, until golden brown and crispy. Remove from oil and place on a paper towel to absorb any excess oil and season immediately.

Part 4: Garnish

| 2 cups | honey | 240 mL |

In a small pot over medium heat, simmer the honey and reduce by 30% or for 10 minutes. While warm, drizzle pools of honey over the open spaces on the serving plate.

Baked White Asparagus Parcels

Serves 4

Butter-baked white asparagus—simply great cooked either in the oven or on the barbecue. If you can't find white asparagus, use green.

4 Tbsp.	melted unsalted butter	60 mL
24	spears white asparagus, peeled	24
¼ cup	kosher salt or table salt	60 mL
¼ cup	white sugar	60 mL
2	oranges, juice of	2
2	lemons, juice of	2
2 Tbsp.	chopped fresh chives	30 mL
2 Tbsp.	chopped fresh parsley	30 mL

Preheat the oven to 400°F (200°C). Prepare 4 squares of aluminum foil, 12 x 12 inches (30 cm x 30 cm). Set the foil squares on a baking sheet and place 1 Tbsp. (15 mL) of the butter in the middle of each square. Place 6 asparagus spears on the buttered foil and season with salt, sugar, and citrus juices. Close the top and ends of the parcels securely and bake for 15–20 minutes.

Presentation: Place the parcels on each plate and open just before serving. Sprinkle with chives and parsley.

Confit Vegetables

Serves 4

Garden vegetables tossed in herbs, covered in a good olive oil, and slow-roasted to intensify all those natural sugars—a real wow factor of flavors.

2 cups	olive oil	480 mL
2 Tbsp.	sugar	60 mL
	kosher salt to taste	
1 tsp.	cracked black peppercorns	5 mL
1	large carrot, sliced crosswise	1
4	ripe tomatoes, quartered	4
1	bulb fennel, sliced into ½-inch (1.2-cm) pieces lengthwise	1
1 lb.	asparagus, cut into 1-inch (2.5-cm) pieces	455 g
2	small Bermuda onions, quartered	2
4	cloves garlic, sliced	4
2	yellow peppers, seeded, cut into thick strips	2
1	sprig each of fresh rosemary, basil, thyme, chopped	1

Preheat the oven to 250°F (120°C). Mix the oil, sugar, salt, and pepper and toss the vegetables and herbs in the mixture to coat. Spread on a non-stick baking tray and bake for 30 minutes. For a dinner party, pre-bake the vegetables for 20 minutes and then reheat them for 10 minutes prior to serving.

Lemon Caper Relish

Makes 1½ cups (360 mL)

For a true lemon explosion, this is it! It's great with my Olaf's Schnitzel Stack, page 119, and the Grilled Lemon Paillard of Turkey, page 136. It's also fantastic with grilled fish or shellfish, poultry, red meats, and vegetables. It's like a small salad of lemon fillets with capers and shallots. You only need a little to make a real wow!

3	lemons, juice of	3
1 tsp.	Dijon mustard	5 mL
¼ tsp.	white pepper	1.2 mL
½ cup	olive oil	120 mL
3	lemons, peeled, seedless segments	3
¼ cup	drained capers	60 mL
1	shallot, finely diced	1
1 Tbsp.	chopped fresh chervil	15 mL
½ cup	chopped fresh Italian parsley	120 mL
	salt to taste	

In a small bowl, place the lemon juice, mustard, and pepper and slowly whisk in the olive oil until it is lightly emulsified and will coat the back of the spoon. Fold in the rest of the ingredients and season with salt.

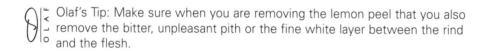 Olaf's Tip: Make sure when you are removing the lemon peel that you also remove the bitter, unpleasant pith or the fine white layer between the rind and the flesh.

Pineapple Sauerkraut

Makes 3 cups (720 mL)

A fruity twist on sauerkraut. Serve with Grilled Smoked Pork Chops, page 128, or with a simple farmer's sausage on a bun!

1	medium onion, sliced	1
1 cup	double-smoked bacon*, rind removed, diced	240 mL
1 Tbsp.	unsalted butter	15 mL
½ cup	cider vinegar (or champagne vinegar)	120 mL
1	1-lb. (455-g) can sauerkraut, drained	1
1	ripe pineapple, peeled and diced	1
1½ cups	dry white wine	360 mL
2	bay leaves	2
½ tsp.	ground cloves	2.5 mL
⅓ cup	sugar	80 mL
¼ tsp.	white pepper	1.2 mL

*See Glossary, page 202.

In a medium pot, sweat the onions and bacon in butter over medium heat until both are soft and translucent. Deglaze with the vinegar and simmer for 3 minutes. Add the remaining ingredients. Reduce heat and simmer for 30 minutes while preparing rest of meal. Keeps well in the refrigerator for 3 days.

Warm Potato Salad

Serves 4

A southern-Germany-style potato salad that could work by itself, or with fish, pork, or sausage. It looks colorful and tastes great!

4	medium Yukon Gold potatoes, unpeeled, whole	4
½ tsp.	caraway seeds	2.5 mL
1 tsp.	sugar	5 mL
1 Tbsp.	salt	15 mL
¾ cup	Chicken Stock (page 21), or store-purchased	180 mL
1 Tbsp.	cornstarch	15 mL
½ cup	cold water	120 mL
1 cup	double-smoked bacon*, rind removed, finely diced	240 mL
1½ cups	combined and very finely diced leeks, carrot, onion	360 mL
⅓ cup	white wine vinegar	80 mL
½ cup	chopped fresh chives	120 mL
¼ cup	chopped fresh parsley	60 mL
	salt and black pepper to taste	
	*See Glossary, page 202.	

In a large pot, over medium heat, bring to a boil the potatoes, caraway seeds, sugar, and salt in enough water to cover the potatoes. Cook for 35 minutes or until you can insert a paring knife easily into the potatoes. Drain the potatoes and, while still warm, peel and dice them into ½-inch (1.2-cm) cubes.

Bring the chicken stock to a boil and mix the cornstarch with water and add to the stock, cooking until it coats the back of a spoon.

Sauté the smoked bacon and remove. In the drippings, quickly wilt the leek, carrot, and onion until translucent. Toss together with the potatoes and bacon, and add the vinegar.

Combine with the stock and add the herbs and seasonings. It can be served warm or cold. Keeps well in the refrigerator for 3 days.

 Olaf's Tip: Preparing the potatoes with the skins on lets the potatoes retain their starches and helps the dressing stick.

Roast Pork Rack Chops with Maple and Dark Beer Sauce (page 126)

Roast Duckling with Red Grapefruit and Green Peppercorn Sauce (page 138)

"A Study of Parsnips" (page 154)

Tower of Blue Cheese Donuts on Vanilla Pears (page 170)

Mandarin Sticky Cake with Brown Sugar Glaze (page 194)

Sun, Moon, and Stars (page 176)

Cheese Dishes

The cheese course, another classic from the old school of dining, provides the diner with what is called the "stomach closing." A menu of seven courses contains some kind of cheese dish that tells your guests "this feast is over —it's time to sit back and relax."

Cheese is fascinating for the way Mother Nature takes raw ingredients, lets bacteria be a good thing, and ends up with such a variety of products.

In my years of apprenticeship, I was taught to appreciate the fine cheeses of the world. It was sometimes my job to go to the train station to receive our delivery of cheeses from the renowned cheese house in Paris: Androuet. The handling of these fine products included learning about storing, presentation, and how to give them the truly special attention they deserve. With cheese as the highlight, the following dishes are simple, flavorful, nutritious, and require only the addition of a light fruit accompaniment and/or a variety or breads, crackers, or crisps.

One of the first colleagues with whom I worked was Bernd (a.k.a. Bernie) Siener from Frankfurt. My friend taught me a love, appreciation, and respect for unpasteurized cheeses. These have a fuller, more natural raw taste but are not available in Canada at all. Still we have our own fantastic cheeses in Canada from blue cheese, triple cream cheese, and aged cheddar, to goat's cheese. With our great lands and dairies and the expertise of some imported cheese-makers from around the world, we too can make great cheeses that are comparable to the world's best.

Here are a few ideas on how to bring cheese to your table. Whether it be a savory or a sweet sensation, the pleasures of creating a simple cheese course can bring a spectacular end to a magnificent meal.

Oka Cheese Soufflé
with a Rhubarb Riesling Relish

Serves 4

Every chef should have a spring cheese course—this is mine! Wilted rhubarb in Riesling syrup makes a great side dish, or you can use it with cheese, pound cake, ice cream, or vanilla pudding.

Part 1: Rhubarb Riesling Relish
Makes 4¼ cups (1 L)

1 cup	honey	240 mL
1	vanilla bean, split and scraped	1
1	lemon, juice and zest of	1
1½ cups	Riesling wine	360 mL
3 cups	diced rhubarb, fresh or frozen	720 mL

In a medium pot over medium heat, place the honey, vanilla bean marrow, lemon juice and zest, and the Riesling wine. Simmer for 15 minutes until the total mixture is reduced by 50% to a syrup. Remove from the heat and fold in the rhubarb. Return to the heat just long enough to soften the rhubarb. Chill until ready to use. Can be stored in the refrigerator for up to one week.

Part 2: Cheese Soufflé

½ cup	melted unsalted butter	120 mL
½ cup	flour	120 mL
¼ cup	unsalted butter	60 mL
1	small onion, coarsely chopped	1
⅓ cup	flour	80 mL
2½ cups	whole milk	600 mL
1	small bay leaf	1
5	cracked white peppercorns	5

½ tsp.	nutmeg	2.5 mL
	salt and white pepper to taste	
3	large egg yolks, beaten	3
⅔ cup	grated Oka cheese	160 mL
⅛ cup	Parmesan cheese	30 mL
3	large egg whites	3

Preheat the oven to 375°F (190°C). Prepare eight 4-oz. (113-g) ramekins, or other ovenproof dishes or molds, by brushing them with the melted butter, being sure to cover all surfaces, then dusting with flour. Set aside.

In a medium pot over medium heat, melt the ¼ cup (60 mL) of butter and sweat off the onion until translucent. Remove from the heat and add the flour. Mix well. Return to the heat, and to this warm mixture, whisk in the cold milk, stirring constantly until it is a creamy consistency. Add the bay leaf, peppercorns, and nutmeg and simmer for 20 minutes, stirring occasionally, or until the mixture coats the back of a spoon. Add the salt and pepper. Remove from the heat and whisk in the egg yolks. Strain the mixture through a fine sieve. Fold in the cheeses and let cool to room temperature. In a separate bowl, whisk the egg whites to firm peaks and fold into the cheese mixture.

Fill the prepared ramekins or molds with the mixture. Place them in a 2-inch (5-cm) deep tray. Add warm water to the tray around the ramekins to 1 inch (2.5 cm) deep and bake for 30 minutes. They should be firm to touch and golden brown.

Presentation: Pool the Rhubarb Riesling Relish onto the center of the plate. Remove the soufflés from the ramekins and place in the center of the relish. To add another twist, fold very ripe strawberries into the Rhubarb Riesling Relish.

 Olaf's Tip: A good idea to try: place the empty tray in the oven, set in the prepared dishes and then, using your kettle or a jug with a spout, add the warm water. When finished baking, carefully lift out the ramekins and turn off the oven, leaving the pan inside. When that hot, hot water cools off, then carry it over to the sink to empty. It's a much safer way to deal with a large pan of hot water. For a dinner party, refrigerate the dishes until you are serving your main course, then place in the oven to warm up.

Fresh Cheese Quark Soufflé
on a Blackberry Ragout

Serves 4

This makes a great cheese dessert. It's a wonderful combination of fantastic sour berries and a light, fluffy soufflé. This has the highest difficulty level in the entire book, but don't be afraid—it's a great recipe. You can do it! A real soufflé! You will have to go back into the kitchen after your main entrée, but if you have everything pre-measured, preparation time is just minutes. Have the oven ready and serve immediately. Hot and sweet!

Part 1: Blackberry Ragout

1 pint (2 cups)	blackberries	480 mL
1 cup	water	240 mL
½ cup	icing sugar	120 mL
¼ cup	honey	60 mL
½	lemon, juice of	½

Carefully wash the blackberries in cold water. Set aside half the berries. In a small pot, simmer the rest of the berries and the remaining ingredients for about 7 minutes or until the syrup coats the back of a spoon. Purée in a food processor or blender and strain through a fine mesh strainer into a clean bowl. Fold the rest of the berries into the mixture. Chill until ready to serve.

Part 2: The Soufflé

¼ cup	melted unsalted butter	60 mL
¼ cup	sugar	60 mL
3	large egg yolks	3
1	lemon, juice and zest of	1
1	vanilla bean, split and scraped	1
1 cup	quark*	240 mL
3	large egg whites	3
	*See Glossary, page 203.	

Preheat the oven to 450°F (230°C). Take four 4-oz. (113-g) ovenproof ramekins or other molds or dishes and brush with melted butter, being sure to cover all areas, then dust with sugar. Set aside.

In a chilled bowl, whip half the sugar (⅛ cup/30 mL) and the 3 egg yolks until a light creamy yellow. Fold lemon juice, zest, vanilla marrow, and quark into the egg mixture.

In a separate bowl, whip the egg whites and the remaining ⅛ cup (30 mL) of sugar to stiff peaks. Fold into the quark mixture, being careful to mix well but not to overmix. Fill the ramekins until ¾ full.

Place the ramekins in a 2-inch (5-cm) deep tray and add warm water to the tray to 1 inch (2.5 cm) deep. Bake for 12 minutes until a golden brown and firm to the touch.

Presentation: It is important to walk—not run—your soufflés right from the oven to the table. A soufflé will fall, but should do so slowly at the table while being eaten. Keep the soufflés in the ramekins, placing each one on a doily-lined plate. Put the Blackberry Ragout on the table to be spooned into the center of the soufflé by you or your guests.

Olaf's Tip: Precision is the key to success with a soufflé. Follow this recipe exactly—not an extra drop of water and no uneven dusting on your ramekins. Pay attention to the details and you will impress yourself! For a hot water safety tip, see page 163.

Creamy Onion Camembert
with Sweet and Sour Radish Salad

Serves 6 to 8

This is a velvety-soft cheese that brings out the onion and chive flavors in a nice contrast of sweet and cream. It's very sophisticated when served as an individual-plates cheese course as I have suggested here, or it can be part of a buffet, or a cocktail hors d'oeuvre for guests to dip into.

Part 1: Sweet and Sour Radish Salad

1 tsp.	sugar	5 mL
2 tsp.	honey	10 mL
1 tsp.	lemon juice	5 mL
1 Tbsp.	white vinegar	15 mL
	salt and white pepper to taste	
7	large radishes, finely sliced	7

Whisk the sugar, honey, lemon juice, vinegar, salt, and pepper together. Toss with the radishes. Make at least 2 hours before serving. It will keep refrigerated for up to a week.

Part 2: The Camembert

8 oz.	ripe Camembert cheese, rind on	225 g
½ cup	quark* or cream cheese	120 mL
½ cup	unsalted butter, room temperature	120 mL
¼ cup	finely diced onion	60 mL
1	green onion, finely sliced	1
2 Tbsp.	chopped fresh chives	30 mL
2	large red radishes, shredded	2
	salt and white pepper to taste	
½ tsp.	sweet paprika	2.5 mL
	*See Glossary, page 203.	

Put the whole Camembert, quark, and butter into a mixing bowl and whip until creamy. Fold in the rest of the ingredients.

Presentation: As a plated cheese course, I would place a small mound of Creamy Onion Camembert in the center of the plate with a dollop of Sweet and Sour Radish Salad and a small green salad to the side. Scatter the plate with some finely sliced green onions. Serve with your choice of bagel chips, crackers, flatbreads, bread sticks, or pumpernickel.

Olaf's Tip: This is a whipped cheese mixture, so use an electric mixer with a mixing paddle to blend. A food processor would make all the ingredients too finely chopped.

Three Point Cambozola Cheese Tartlet
with Port Wine-Spiked Figs

Makes 16 tarts/Serves 8

I love Cambozola cheese! You will see it in many of my recipes. Because of its rich, creamy texture, it has to be one of the best cheeses ever, giving a light accent of blue cheese in the finishing flavor. These scrumptious tarts are best served to your guests right from the oven to get the full benefit of flavors.

Part 1: Port Wine-Spiked Figs

¼ cup	sugar	60 mL
⅛ tsp.	ground cloves	.5 mL
1	cinnamon stick	1
¼ cup	water	60 mL
2 cups	port wine	480 mL
8	dried figs, cut into quarters	8

Bring the first five ingredients to a simmer in a medium pot over medium heat for 3 minutes or until thickened and the liquid coats the back of a spoon. Fold in the figs and store in the refrigerator until ready to use. Remove the cinnamon stick before serving.

Part 2: Cheese Tartlet

1¼ cups	flour	300 mL
¼ cup	sugar	60 mL
½ tsp.	salt	2.5 mL
¾ cup	cold unsalted butter	180 mL
1	large egg, beaten	1
¾ lb.	Cambozola cheese, crumbled	340 g

Preheat the oven to 350°F (175°C). In a mixing bowl, toss the flour, sugar, and salt together. Slowly blend in the butter with an electric mixer or by hand until it's an oatmeal-like consistency. Mix in the egg until the dough forms a ball. Wrap in plastic wrap and chill for at least 30 minutes. Roll out the pastry to ¼-inch (.6-cm) thick and cut into 3-inch (7.5-cm) circles with a cookie cutter or a glass. Pinch in 3 corners of each circle to form small dishes or tartlets. Fill in the tartlet shells with the cheese. Bake for 10–12 minutes, or until golden brown.

Presentation: On small plates, place two tartlets and surround with a couple of dollops of Port Wine-Spiked Figs. You can dust the plate lightly with ground cinnamon and garnish with lemon balm or mint sprigs.

Olaf's Tip: Although Cambozola is readily available, you can substitute Camembert or Brie if you are not a fan of blue cheese.

Tower of Blue Cheese Donuts on Vanilla Pears

Makes about ten 2-oz. (57-g) doughnuts

You can't get more ordinary than a doughnut. But this recipe takes the ordinary and gives it a twist into something really fantastic, filled with the unexpected: blue cheese! Don't like blue cheese? Use Brie or cheddar!

Part 1: Vanilla Pear Marmalade

½ cup	unsalted butter	120 mL
4	pears, peeled and sliced	4
1	lemon, juice and zest of	1
1	vanilla bean, split and scraped	1
2 Tbsp.	honey	30 mL
1 cup	white wine	240 mL

In a small pot on medium heat, lightly brown the butter. Add the sliced pears and lightly roast until brown. Add the lemon juice and zest, vanilla marrow, honey, and white wine. Simmer for 10 minutes or until the mixture has a marmalade texture. Store in the refrigerator until ready to serve, for a maximum of 3 days.

Part 2: Blue Cheese Donuts

1 cup	blue cheese, room temperature	240 mL
½ cup	cream cheese, room temperature	120 mL
1 oz.	fresh yeast	28 g
¼ cup	whole milk, warmed	60 mL
2	large eggs	2
2	large egg yolks	2
1½ Tbsp.	sugar	22 mL
¼ cup	milk	60 mL
1 cup	flour	240 mL
2 Tbsp.	unsalted butter, room temperature	30 mL

½	lemon, zest of	½
½ oz.	rum	14 g
1 tsp.	vanilla extract	5 mL
¼ tsp.	salt	1.2 mL
1	large egg yolk	1
¼ cup	milk	60 mL
	icing sugar for topping	
	vegetable oil for frying	

Mix the blue cheese and cream cheese together and set aside. Sprinkle the yeast over ¼ cup (60 mL) of warm milk. Set aside but do not refrigerate. Beat the eggs, egg yolks, sugar, ¼ cup (60 mL) milk, flour, butter, lemon zest, rum, vanilla, and salt until light and fluffy and doubled in volume. Slowly fold in the yeast and milk mixture by hand. Rest in a warm area—about 85°F (29°C) is ideal—until the dough rises, about 30 minutes. Turn the dough out of the bowl onto a work surface and punch down. Roll out the dough to ¾-inch (1.9-cm) thickness and cut twenty 3-inch (7.5-cm) circles using a cookie cutter or a glass. Place 10 of these circles on a parchment-lined cookie sheet and place 1 Tbsp. (15 mL) of the cheese mixture in the middle of each circle. Make an egg wash with the egg yolk and ¼ cup (60 mL) milk and paint the edges with it. Place another circle on top of each circle. Pinch to seal. Proof the doughnuts again by covering with a clean cloth and resting in a warm place to rise again, about 30 minutes.

Pour about 2 inches (5 cm) of vegetable oil into a deep pot or deep fryer. Fry the doughnuts, a few at a time, at 350°F (175°C) for 3 minutes on each side, or until golden brown. Remove from the oil and place onto paper towels. Dust immediately with icing sugar. Don't allow the oil to get too hot or they will burn quickly.

Presentation: Pool the Vanilla Pear Marmalade into the center of each plate. Set a doughnut on the pear mixture.

 Olaf's Tip: If you don't have a deep fryer, use a deep pot to fry in, as deep-frying requires the item to be covered in oil to cook properly. A deep pot allows you to use less oil than you would need in a saucepan and prevents splattering of the hot oil.

Oven-Roasted Vanilla Pears
Stuffed with Brie Nut Crumble

Serves 4

Candy-roasted pears oozing with melted Brie cheese and crunchy nuts. A fantastic combo! You can easily substitute the pears with apples, peaches, or plums.

Part 1: Vanilla Pears

4	large ripe pears	4
1	vanilla bean, split and scraped	1
1 Tbsp.	cinnamon	15 mL
1 cup	maple syrup	240 mL
4 cups	white wine	960 mL
1	lemon, zest of	1

Peel the pears, cut in half lengthwise, and using a small spoon or a melon baller, remove the cores. Make a fine slice on the outside (bottom) of the pear so that it will sit flat on the baking tray. In a medium pot, simmer the rest of the ingredients and poach the pears for 10 minutes until tender. Remove the pears onto a non-stick baking tray.

Part 2: Nut Crumble

¼ cup	unsalted butter, room temperature	60 mL
½ cup	flour	120 mL
½ cup	each of ground pecans, hazelnuts, and pistachios	120 mL
½ cup	quick-cooking oats	120 mL
¼ cup	brown sugar	60 mL
1 tsp.	nutmeg	5 mL

Toss together in a mixing bowl until a crumbly consistency.

Part 3: Stuffing the Pears

| 8 | 1-oz. (28-g) pieces Brie cheese, rind on | 8 |

Preheat the oven to 350°F (175°C). To assemble the pears, take the tender, hollowed-out pears, fill the hollow with Brie, and cover them with the crumble. Bake for 5 minutes or until the crumble is golden brown.

Part 4: Warm Buckwheat Thyme Honey

| 2 cups | buckwheat honey | 480 mL |
| 2 | sprigs fresh thyme | 2 |

In a small pot, simmer the honey and thyme for 5 minutes. Remove the sprigs of thyme. Keep warm.

Presentation: Place a stuffed pear in the middle of each plate and drizzle the honey around the pear.

The Grand Finale: Desserts

Most of us have a secret longing; mine was to be a pastry chef. I gave it considerable thought, but it required another two and a half years of training on top of my just-completed three-year program. It simply didn't pan out for me, but I spent as much time as I could in the pastry shop. In the hotel in Germany, where I apprenticed, our pastry shop was very fortunate in having three master pastry chefs in one shop . . . can you imagine the delicacies! The hotel was of such a high caliber that, fortunately for me, everything was made from scratch—cakes, ice creams, croissants, chocolate truffles, and especially breads. The learning was there for the taking and, believe me, I took!

I recall one of the chefs teaching us his unique methods as a reward, in order to motivate the young apprentices. I enjoyed his teachings and acquired a strong understanding of and respect for the art of "patisserie." This collection of recipes is rooted in my classical kitchen training, but as you will see, I've given them my stamp—fun, fresh, and twisted!

The dessert! The grand finale! It's the last dish of the menu and provides the final memory of the evening, so make it a lasting impression. Even if you are intimidated by the pictures or the long instructions in these recipes, give them a try. Pick one and work at it. The result will be well worth it!

Rhubarb Cake

Makes a 9-x 13-inch (23-cm x 33-cm) cake

Use fresh rhubarb if possible (check your neighbor's backyard or a farmer's market), or frozen will work too. This dessert will become one of your family's favorites. Freeze the rhubarb and enjoy this great cake all year long.

1½ cups	brown sugar	360 mL
½ cup	oil	120 mL
1	large egg	1
1 cup	sour cream	240 mL
2 cups	flour	480 mL
1 tsp.	baking soda	5 mL
1 tsp.	nutmeg	5 mL
1 tsp.	cinnamon	5 mL
½ tsp.	salt	2.5 mL
4 cups	diced rhubarb	960 mL

Topping

½ cup	brown sugar	120 mL
1 Tbsp.	butter	15 mL
1 tsp.	cinnamon	5 mL
½ cup	chopped walnuts	120 mL

Preheat the oven to 350°F (175°C). Cream the sugar and oil together. Add the egg and sour cream. Mix in the rest of the ingredients. Pour into a greased 9-x 13-inch (23-cm x 33-cm) pan.

In a small bowl, combine the topping ingredients and sprinkle on top of the cake. Bake for 45–50 minutes or until a cake tester comes out clean.

Presentation: If you want to fancy up this recipe, make the Vanilla Cream Sauce, page 28, and pool the sauce onto a plate. Top with a piece of cake and scatter with any seasonal berries for garnish.

 Olaf's Tip: If parts of the rhubarb seem old or tough, peel it with a vegetable peeler to prevent a stringy texture.

Sun, Moon, and Stars

Serves 4

It looks amazing. It also looks hard to do! But it's not, really—the presentation is the most challenging part. Follow my instructions for the mousse and then play with the chocolate decoration. They're not as tricky as they appear. Come on! Try it!

Part 1: White Chocolate Mousse

3	sheets gelatin*	3
2 cups	35% cream	480 mL
2	large eggs	2
2	large egg yolks	2
1/3 cup	sugar	80 mL
1 oz.	crème de cacao liqueur	28 mL
1 oz.	white rum	28 mL
6 oz.	white chocolate, coarsely chopped	170 g
1 cup	chocolate wafer or cookie crumbs	240 mL
	*See Glossary, page 202.	

You will also need:

4-oz. (113-g) ramekins or other small, low dishes, perhaps a coffee cup

3-inch (7.5-cm) round cookie cutter

2-inch (5-cm) point-to-point star cookie cutter

1 large half-moon cookie cutter

edible gold flakes (available at cake supply stores)

plastic overhead transparency

parchment paper

plastic wrap

To prepare the dishes, place a piece of plastic wrap over each dish and, using your fingers, press the wrap down into the bowl to form a lining. Leave enough extra wrap around the top to cover up the dish after filling. Chill the dishes until ready to use.

Submerge the gelatin in enough cold water to cover and set aside. Whip the cream to medium peaks and refrigerate. In a double boiler or a stainless steel bowl over a pot of simmering water, whisk the eggs, egg yolks, and sugar until ribbons form. Remove the gelatin from the cold water and melt in the warm egg mixture. Transfer the egg mixture to a large bowl. Again in the double boiler, melt the white chocolate slowly over medium heat, stirring constantly. When melted, mix well into the egg mixture. This mixture may be quite thick but will loosen as you slowly use a whisk to blend in the crème de cacao and rum. When the mixture is room temperature, fold in the whipped cream. Spoon the mousse into the chilled, lined ramekins and cover with the remaining plastic wrap and freeze for at least 4 hours. Set aside the chocolate wafer crumbs until ready for assembly.

Part 2: The Sauces (Coulis)
Color One: Mango Coulis

2	ripe mangos	2
1 cup	water	240 mL
1 cup	icing sugar	240 mL
1	lemon, juice of	1

continued on next page

Peel the mangos and cut into large pieces. Simmer the water, icing sugar, and lemon juice until syrup-like. Add the mango pieces and simmer until the fruit is tender. In a food processor or blender, purée until smooth. Strain through a fine mesh strainer and chill.

Color Two: Raspberry Coulis

2 cups	raspberries	480 mL
½ cup	water	120 mL
½ cup	icing sugar	120 mL
½	lemon, juice of	½

Wash the raspberries and drain. Simmer the water, sugar, and lemon juice until it has a syrup-like consistency. Add the raspberries. Purée in a food processor or blender and strain through a fine mesh strainer. Chill.

Color Three: Light Mango Coulis

½ cup	mango coulis (from Color Two above)	120 mL
1 Tbsp.	sour cream	15 mL

Mix together and chill.

Part 3: Shooting Stars

1½ lbs.	semi-sweet dark chocolate	680 g
½ lb.	white chocolate	225 g

Cut the chocolate into pieces. In a double boiler or stainless steel bowl over a pot of simmering water, melt the semi-sweet chocolate. Melt it slowly, stirring frequently. Once this chocolate has all melted, quickly remove it from the heat and allow to stand for 5 minutes. Repeat the process for the white chocolate.

To achieve shiny chocolate, you will need 2 transparency sheets, 8- x 11-inches (20-cm x 28-cm). Place the first sheet on a tray or baking sheet, and pour a thin layer, about ⅛-inch (.3 cm) thick of semi-sweet dark chocolate onto the sheet and let set. Do the same with the white chocolate on the other sheet.

From the semi-sweet sheet, and using the round cookie cutter, cut 6 circles, allowing 2 for breakage. To make the arches, again from the dark chocolate, use a knife to cut out 8 arches (refer to the color photo between pages 160 and 161), about 6 inches long and 1 inch wide (15 cm x 2.5 cm).

From the white chocolate, and using the cookie cutters, cut out the half moons and stars. (To make the eyes on the moon, drop a tiny circle of dark chocolate onto the moons.) Glue the half moons, using melted chocolate, onto the four dark-chocolate circles. Glue the stars onto the arches giving the illusion of shooting stars.

Take the excess white chocolate and remelt it. Use it to "draw" lines down the length of the dark chocolate arches to resemble shooting star tails. Sprinkle the tails with gold flakes.

Presentation

1. Finish off the mousse by removing the dishes from the freezer, removing all the plastic wrap, and rolling the sides of the mousse in the chocolate wafer crumbs, leaving the top and bottom plain. Place on a tray and put back in the refrigerator for about 1 hour to thaw.

2. To make the sun: in the center of a chilled plate, make a 3-inch (7.5-cm) circle with the Color One: Mango Coulis. Around that circle, make a ring with the Color Two: Raspberry Coulis, and another ring around that with the Color Three: Light Mango Coulis. Starting at the center, take a toothpick and draw through the three rings to make a sun-like pattern showing the "rays."

3. Using a spatula, carefully place the mousse into the center of the coulis sun pattern.

4. Use your already prepared chocolate work to complete the look!

OLAF Olaf's Tip: Use the side of the chocolate that is peeled directly from the transparency sheet.

Ice Cream Candies

Makes about 12 candies of each of 4 colors

How different can you get—marzipan and ice cream dressed up to go out for dinner! This is a knock'em-dead dessert that can be made several days in advance and assembled while your guests are retiring to coffee and liqueurs. I have used natural ingredients to color the marzipan. This adds richness and flavor, but they can be substituted with artificial food coloring if you really want a shortcut.

Part 1: Marzipan Base

| 1 lb. | marzipan (almond paste) | 455 g |

Colorings

¼ cup	grenadine syrup (red)	60 mL
1 Tbsp.	saffron powder (yellow)	15 mL
1 Tbsp.	cocoa powder (brown)	15 mL
¼ cup	creme de menthe (green)	60 mL
2 cups	icing sugar	480 mL

Evenly divide the marzipan into 4 small bowls and add one of the listed ingredients per bowl to make the four colors. If the mixes are too wet, add some icing sugar to make them a dough-like consistency. Using icing sugar on your work surface to prevent the marzipan from sticking, roll out the colored marzipan to ⅛-inch (.3-cm) thick and cut into different shapes using an assortment of small bite-sized cookie cutters. Place on a parchment-paper-lined tray and chill.

 Olaf's Tip: Marzipan or almond paste can be purchased at cake supply stores, bulk food supply stores, or ask your local baker to sell you some.

Part 2: Ice Cream

1 cup	vanilla ice cream	240 mL
1 cup	chocolate ice cream	240 mL
1 cup	raspberry sorbet	240 mL
1 cup	mango sorbet	240 mL

Place the ice creams and sorbets into the refrigerator for half an hour prior to using. Put the ice creams and sorbets into piping bags, one at a time, and pipe swirls onto the marzipan shapes. Place on a serving dish and place in the freezer.

Part 3: Chocolate Ornaments

2 cups	white chocolate	480 mL
2 cups	semi-sweet dark chocolate	480 mL

Melt the white chocolate over a double boiler. When melted, use a fine-tipped pastry bag to drizzle it into decorative patterns onto parchment-paper-lined trays or baking sheets. The designs can be such things as initials, musical notes, fine mesh, spirals, etc. Repeat with the semi-sweet dark chocolate. Place in the freezer to harden. Peel off the paper to place on the "candies."

Presentation: Leave the ice cream and marzipan "candies" in the freezer until ready to use. Place them on a large decorative platter and top them with your chocolate artwork and/or some fruit/nut garnishes. Fresh raspberries, blueberries, and blackberries are very colorful garnishes or try using pistachios, hazelnuts, or almonds. Either serve the candies with your dessert, or better still, bring out the serving dish after the dessert for a really grand finale.

Swiss Muesli Cocktail

Makes 12 cups (3 L)

For breakfast or dessert? I don't know. You decide. Cold cereal is not just for breakfast anymore. This gives an elegant variation to plain brunch buffets or for an impressive morning-after meal!

2 cups	quark*	480 mL
2 cups	plain yogurt	480 mL
¼ cup	liquid honey	60 mL
¼ cup	sugar	60 mL
2	oranges, juice of	2
1	lemon, juice of	1
1 Tbsp.	vanilla extract	15 mL
1 cup	whole milk	240 mL
1 cup	quick-cooking oats	240 mL
½ cup	hazelnut crumbs	120 mL
2	Granny Smith apples, unpeeled, diced	2
2	ripe bananas, sliced	2
1⅔ cups	35% cream, whipped	400 mL

*See Glossary, page 203.

In a large bowl, whisk the quark, yogurt, honey, sugar, citrus juices, vanilla, and milk. Fold in the oats, half the nuts, fruits, and then the whipped cream. Set aside half of the hazelnut crumbs and a few pieces of the fruit for the garnish.

Garnish

	honey for topping	
1 pint (2 cups)	strawberries	480 mL
¼ cup	hazelnut crumbs	60 mL

Portion the muesli into serving dishes and garnish with honey, reserved fruit, strawberries, and reserved hazelnuts.

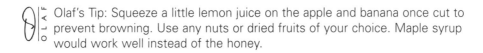 Olaf's Tip: Squeeze a little lemon juice on the apple and banana once cut to prevent browning. Use any nuts or dried fruits of your choice. Maple syrup would work well instead of the honey.

Millennium Champagne Jelly

Serves 4

Jelly brings back childhood memories of the wiggly jiggly stuff, but this has definitely been twisted for adults. Great as an "intermezzo" before the main course as we did at On The Curve Restaurant in Mississauga, Ontario, for the New Year's Eve 2001 celebration.

1½ cups	champagne	360 mL
5	sheets gelatin*	5
1	lime, juice of	1
½	orange, juice and zest of	½
1	lemon, juice and zest of	1
1	stalk lemongrass, chopped	1
1	vanilla bean, split and scraped	1
½ cup	liquid honey	120 mL
1½ cups	late-harvest Riesling wine	360 mL
2 cups	mixed raspberries, strawberries, and blueberries	480 mL

*See Glossary, page 202.

Chill the champagne. Soak the gelatin sheets in cold water to dissolve.

In a small pot, simmer the three citrus juices and zests, lemongrass, vanilla bean marrow, honey, and Riesling wine for 5 minutes. Drain the gelatin sheets and melt them in the warm syrup. Through a fine mesh strainer, strain this mixture, then pour into a large chilled bowl and refrigerate for 1 hour, or until set. Before serving, use a whisk to break up the jelly, then add the champagne. Pour into wine glasses, old-fashioned champagne glasses, or margarita glasses and top with fresh berries.

 Olaf's Tip: You can get lemongrass stalks from an Asian market, and some grocery stores. It is a very brittle stalk, so chop carefully with a sharp knife or cleaver, or even try a clean pair of garden shears. Don't worry about it crunching up your jelly; it is used to flavor the liquid but then strained away, leaving your jelly crystal clear and flavorful. If you want the bubbles without the champagne, use sparkling fruit juice.

Warm Rice Pudding
with Grilled Vanilla White Peaches

Serves 4

Rice pudding is a tasty comfort food, a favorite of many, but boy do the grilled peaches add a sweet twist for the taste buds. This is a fantastic late-summer dessert, just when the peaches are picked from the orchards.

Part 1: Grilled Vanilla White Peaches

4	white peaches, ripe but not soft	4
2 oz.	brandy	57 mL
4 oz.	peach schnapps	113 mL
½ cup	water	120 mL
½ cup	maple syrup	120 mL
½ cup	honey	120 mL
1	vanilla bean, split and scraped	1
1	lemon, juice of	1

Carefully cut each peach in half and remove the pit. On a hot, clean barbecue grill, place the peach halves, cut-side down. Grill for 2 minutes, then rotate each peach 90° (so you get a nice grill mark on the flesh) and cook for 2 minutes more. Flip the peach over and continue to grill as before, but with the skin-side down. Do not close the lid as this will overcook the peaches.

In a small pot, simmer the brandy, schnapps, water, maple syrup, honey, vanilla bean marrow, and lemon juice for 10 minutes to a thick syrup. In a bowl, cover the peaches with the syrup and allow them to chill for about 4 hours.

Part 2: Rice Pudding

¼ cup	unsalted butter	60 mL
1	vanilla bean, split and scraped	1
1 cup	arborio rice	240 mL
¾ cup	sugar	180 mL
5 cups	whole milk	1.2 L
¼ tsp.	salt	1.2 mL
¼ cup	cold unsalted butter, cubed	60 mL
1 cup	35% cream, whipped	240 mL

In a medium pot over medium heat, melt the butter and sauté the vanilla bean marrow, arborio rice, and sugar. Stir in 1 cup (240 mL) of the milk and allow the rice mixture to absorb it, about 2–3 minutes. Continue to stir and add the milk 1 cup (240 mL) at a time until it has all been absorbed and the rice is tender. Remove from the heat. Season with salt and stir in the cold butter cubes. Store in the refrigerator until ready to serve. When ready, warm slightly on the stovetop and fold in the whipped cream.

Presentation: In a tall wine glass, or a dish of your choice, place a scoop of the warm rice pudding, top with a peach, and drizzle with the syrup.

 Olaf's Tip: White peaches are preferable, but their season is short, so they may not be available. Local ripe peaches will do!

Lemon Parfait Brûlée
on a Lemongrass Jelly Sauce

Makes 8 generous servings

Lemon is always great and refreshing, but twice in one dessert makes this twice the dessert in one!

Part 1: Lemon Parfait Brûlée

1	sheet gelatin*	1
6	large egg yolks	6
1 cup	sugar	240 mL
1 oz.	citrus vodka	28 g
3	lemons, juice and zest of	3
1 2/3 cups	35% cream, whipped to soft peaks	400 mL
1/2 cup	icing sugar	120 mL
	*See Glossary, page 202.	

Prepare eight 4-oz. (113-g) ramekin dishes by lining them with plastic wrap. Dissolve the gelatin sheet in enough cold water to cover.

Using a double boiler or stainless steel bowl over a simmering pot of water, combine the egg yolks, sugar, vodka, lemon juice, and zest. Whisk until thick and fluffy, about 5 minutes. Remove the gelatin sheet and place into the warm egg mixture. Place the mixture in a mixing bowl and mix at medium-high speed until fluffy and smooth. Fold the whipped cream into the egg mixture. Ladle the mixture into the dishes lined with plastic wrap and freeze for about 3 hours.

Part 2: Lemongrass Jelly Sauce

4	sheets gelatin	4
1 cup	sugar	240 mL
1 cup	honey	240 mL
2 cups	water	480 mL
1	stalk lemongrass, finely diced	1
4	lemons, juice of, plus zest of 2 lemons	4

Dissolve the 4 sheets of gelatin in enough cold water to cover and set aside until needed. Simmer the sugar, honey, water, and lemongrass on medium heat for about 5 minutes until it reaches a syrupy consistency. Add the lemon juice and lemon zest and continue simmering for another 5 minutes, stirring frequently. Remove from heat and allow to cool for 5 minutes. Add the gelatin sheets and gently stir until dissolved. Strain the mixture through a fine mesh strainer into a bowl and let sit in the refrigerator for at least an hour until set. When ready to serve, use a strong whisk or a fork to whisk the jelly to break it down to a thickened sauce.

Part 3: Garnish

2	oranges	2
2	pink grapefruits	2
2	limes	2
2 Tbsp.	sugar	30 mL
2 oz.	orange liqueur	57 mL

Peel and segment the oranges, grapefruit, and limes so that only the fleshy part of each fruit remains. In a bowl, dissolve the sugar in the orange liqueur and gently toss in the citrus segments.

Presentation: Remove the parfaits from the freezer about half an hour before serving and place them on individual plates. When ready to serve, dust the parfaits with icing sugar, then take a small propane torch and heat the surface of the parfaits until it looks like a crystalized candy. Place equal amounts of the mixed fruits around the bottoms of the parfaits. Spoon puddles of the lemongrass jelly around the parfait and fruit.

Olaf's Tip: The gelatin in the parfait will reduce any ice crystals. For information on lemongrass, see page 183. A large mold could be used and the brûlée scooped into dessert or wine glasses with Lemongrass Jelly Sauce in the bottom and a drizzle on the top.

Using a blow torch is the only way to really do this unless you have a salamander stove. Read the manufacturer's directions. Let the tip of the flame caramelize the sugar crust on top.

Summer Red Berry Pot
with Honey-Spiked Sour Cream and Pistachios

Serves 8

Summer berries married in red wine and tapioca with a tasty sour cream topping. This is a really simple, clean dessert, perfect for a summer gathering when it is just too hot for anything else. This has the added benefit of being able to store the leftover berry pot in the refrigerator or even in the freezer for when you need more. It's equally nice when served with a good vanilla ice cream as an extra-special sundae!

Part 1: Berry Pot

2 Tbsp.	tapioca	30 mL
2 cups	cranberry juice	480 mL
4	sheets gelatin*	4
1½ cups	red wine	360 mL
½ cup	sugar	120 mL
½ cup	liquid honey	120 mL
1	cinnamon stick	1
3 oz.	rum	85 mL
	*See Glossary, page 202.	

All of the following berries can be purchased fresh or frozen.

1 cup	strawberries	240 mL
1 cup	raspberries	240 mL
1 cup	red currants	240 mL
1 cup	pitted cherries, frozen or canned	240 mL
1 cup	blueberries	240 mL

Wash and hull all the fruits. Soak the tapioca in ½ cup (120 mL) of the cranberry juice and set aside. Submerge the gelatin sheets in cold water and set aside. Over medium heat in a large pot, bring the wine, the remaining 1½ cups (360 mL) cranberry juice, sugar, honey, cinnamon stick, and rum to a boil. Drain the gelatin sheet and add it to the tapioca and cranberry juice mixture. Add this mixture to the pot and continue to simmer for 7–10 minutes until the tapioca is clear and tender. Add all the berries and simmer for 10–15 minutes more.

Part 2: Honey-Spiked Sour Cream

1 cup	sour cream	240 mL
½ cup	liquid honey	120 mL
1	vanilla bean, split and scraped	1
1 cup	35% cream, whipped	240 mL
¼ cup	finely chopped pistachios	60 mL

In a small bowl, mix the sour cream, honey, and vanilla marrow, then fold in the whipped cream. Store in the refrigerator until ready to serve.

Presentation: Portion the berry mixture into 6-oz. (170-g) wine glasses or small martini glasses. Place on a doily-lined plate to serve. Add a large dollop of Honey Spiked Sour Cream to the top of berries. To really make an impact, sprinkle with the pistachio nuts and top with a fresh strawberry.

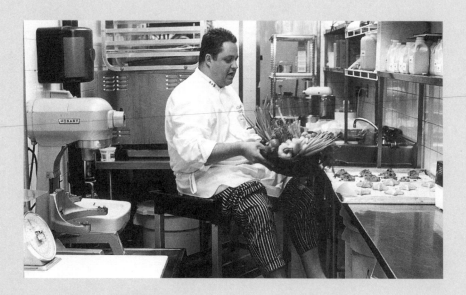

Caramelized Bananas
with Riesling Foam

Serves 4

If you haven't tried caramelized bananas then you don't know what you're missing. This is a special treat that you cook just before serving so that the banana and nutty brown bourbon caramel sauce are warm and fragrant. Serve it with the Riesling Foam that has the texture of a mousse but dances on your tongue.

Part 1: Riesling Foam

3	sheets gelatin*	3
½ cup	Riesling wine	120 mL
¼ cup	sugar	60 mL
4	large egg yolks	4
1 cup	35% cream, whipped	240 mL
	*See Glossary, page 202.	

Dissolve the gelatin in enough cold water to cover. Set aside. In a double boiler or stainless steel bowl, over simmering water, whisk the wine, sugar, and egg yolks until thick ribbons form when drizzled from the whisk. Add the drained gelatin and melt into the mixture. Let this cool to room temperature and then fold in the whipped cream. Store in the refrigerator until ready to serve.

Part 2: Caramelized Bananas

4	bananas, slightly green, halved lengthwise	4
1 cup	macadamia nuts, halved	240 mL
½ cup	butter	120 mL
½ cup	brown sugar	120 mL
2 oz.	bourbon	57 mL
1 cup	35% cream	240 mL
½ cup	cold unsalted butter, cubed	120 mL

In a large non-stick pan on high heat, roast the bananas until brown. When all sides are done, turn down the heat to medium-high, add the nuts and roast until lightly brown. Add the butter until also light brown. Stir in the brown sugar and bourbon and melt for about 3 minutes until it reaches a syrupy consistency. Remove the bananas from the pan and place on individual plates. Add the cream to the pan and reduce by 50%. Remove from the heat and whisk in the cold butter cubes.

Presentation: Place a banana half on the center of the plates. Place the second banana so that it's half leaning on the first banana. Pour the nutty bourbon sauce over. Scoop the Riesling Foam into a ball just like ice cream and place to one side of the bananas.

 Olaf's Tip: Bananas that are overripe will turn mushy under strong heat, so choose ones that are yellow with no black spots.

Oh Chocolate Dreams

Serves 8 to 10

For all you chocolate lovers, this one is for you! It's the ultimate chocolate cake—a moist, delicious cake covered with an incredible shell of rich chocolate. This is so much more sophisticated than regular chocolate cake and frosting; it's a shame to put them in the same category. It's very rich; a one-inch slice is enough at the end of a meal. You may wish you hadn't eaten so much dinner!

Part 1: The Cake

10 oz.	high-quality bittersweet chocolate chunks	285 g
2 oz.	unsweetened chocolate	55 g
1½ cups	unsalted butter	360 mL
1¼ cups	sugar	300 mL
½ cup	finely ground toasted almonds	120 mL
½ cup	flour	120 mL
8	large eggs, separated	8

Preheat the oven to 350°F (175°C). Using a double boiler or stainless steel bowl over simmering water, melt both kinds of chocolate and the butter together. Remove from the heat and whisk in the sugar, almonds, flour, and egg yolks. In a separate bowl, beat the egg whites until they form peaks, but don't make them too stiff or dry. Fold into the chocolate mixture carefully. Butter and flour a 9-inch (23-cm) springform pan and pour in the batter. Important: drop the filled pan on the countertop a couple of times to force air bubbles to the top. Bake for 30–45 minutes, or until a toothpick inserted into the center of the cake comes out clean. The cake should cool for at least an hour until it is room temperature before you make the glaze.

Part 2: The Glaze

¾ cup	35% cream	180 mL
½ lb.	semi-sweet chocolate, coarsely chopped	225 g
½ cup	cold unsalted butter, cubed	120 mL

Bring the cream to a simmer over medium heat and then whisk in the chocolate pieces until melted. Remove from the heat and whisk in the cold butter cubes.

Place the cake on a wire rack that is placed on a baking tray, to catch any drips. Gently pour the glaze over the cake, starting at the center and working outward to the sides until all the sides are covered. As the chocolate eventually stops dripping off the cake, use two big spatulas to gently lift the cake onto a decorative cake plate. Chill until ready to serve.

Presentation: Have a clean, simple presentation—bring to the table for all to see. You could garnish it with a few fresh berries and some good vanilla ice cream.

Olaf's Tip: This cake should be baked in a slow oven to prevent any cracking in the cake. It is unsuitable for baking in a convection oven.

Mandarin Sticky Cake
with Brown Sugar Glaze

Makes a 9- x 13-inch (23-cm x 33-cm) cake, plus leftovers!

For a casual dessert, this cake can be topped with the Brown Sugar Glaze. But to twist it up to another level with a definite wow factor, serve with the Orange Sesame Seed Tuille and decorative sauces. Tuille is a very fine cookie-like wafer that comes in many flavors, to be shaped and formed in any way you want.

Part 1: The Cake

3	10-oz. (284-mL) cans mandarin orange sections, drained	3
2 cups	flour	480 mL
2 cups	sugar	480 mL
2 tsp.	vanilla extract	10 mL
2 tsp.	baking powder	10 mL
½ tsp.	minced ginger	2.5 mL
2	large eggs	2
1 tsp.	salt	5 mL
1 cup	chopped walnuts	240 mL

Preheat the oven to 325°F (165°C). Set aside one can of orange sections for the garnish. In a medium-size bowl, using an electric mixer, combine all the ingredients until well blended. Pour into a parchment-lined 9-x 13-inch (23-cm x 33-cm) pan and bake for 30 minutes, or until a cake tester comes out clean. Let cool in the pan.

Part 2: Brown Sugar Glaze

3 Tbsp.	butter	45 mL
¾ cup	brown sugar	180 mL
3 Tbsp.	milk	45 mL
½ cup	water	120 mL

In a small pot, combine all ingredients and bring to a boil. Simmer for 3 minutes. Pierce the top of the cake with a skewer or toothpick to allow the glaze to soak in. Pour the glaze over the warm cake. After cooling, the cake can then be cut into squares, rounds, triangles, etc. Use the mandarin oranges for garnish.

Part 3: Orange Sesame Seed Tuille

1 cup	sugar	240 mL
½ cup	orange juice	120 mL
½ cup	melted unsalted butter	120 mL
½ cup	mix of black and white sesame seeds*	120 mL
½ cup	flour	120 mL

*White sesame seeds are black sesame seeds after they are peeled. You can purchase them at any supermarket or bulk store.

Preheat the oven to 350°F (175°C). In a bowl, mix the sugar and orange juice. Add the rest of the ingredients and let sit for at least 30 minutes.

Now I want you to really twist this recipe. It is an unexpected method to form the sails, but you'll probably have everything you need in your kitchen!

To form the sails you will need a plastic lid from a large margarine or ice cream container. Free hand, draw and cut out an oval as big as the lid allows, leaving a border of about half an inch (1.2 cm). Set the lid with the oval removed (your stencil) onto a non-stick baking sheet and, as thinly as you can, spread the tuille dough in the stencil. Remove the stencil. Repeat at least 6 more times (extras to allow for breakage). Bake for about 3 minutes. While the wafer is still warm, you will need to cut a 1-inch (2.5-cm) circle about half an inch (1.2 cm) from the top edge. Use a small cookie cutter if you have one. This is a hole for the "mast" to go through. Immediately lay the warm wafer over a rolling pin and allow to cool. Voilà, a sail!

In a small piping bag with a ¼-inch (.6-cm) tip, pipe the rest of the tuille mixture into 4 long sticks for the masts. Bake for 2 minutes and let cool.

Presentation: You are now ready to set sail! Put your mast and sail together by placing the mast through the hole you made in the wafer sail and place on top of a piece of cake and you're off! Bon voyage! If you want to really show off, follow the color photo between pages 160 and 161, and continue with the creativity!

1 recipe	Raspberry Coulis (page 178)	1 recipe
1 recipe	Mango Coulis (page 178)	1 recipe
1 recipe	Chocolate Sauce (page 29)	1 recipe

Using the above sauces, form the sun shape as directed in Sun, Moon, and Stars, page 176. Place the "boat" of cake onto the sun and top with the sail and mast. If you wish, use the above sauces to design the dragon and garnish according to the color photo.

Potato Cake with Caramelized Almonds and Dates

Serves 4, plus leftovers!

This is a flourless cake featuring a very old-fashioned baking technique. You just have to try this and experience the difference. It is as light as air, and all you taste are raisins and brandy. It's a true culinary experience.

Part 1: Potato Cake

3 oz.	brandy	85 mL
¼ cup	raisins (any kind)	60 mL
1¾ lbs.	Yukon Gold potatoes (roughly about 4 large), unpeeled	800 g
6	large eggs, separated	6
⅔ cup	sugar	160 mL
2 tsp.	salt	10 mL

Preheat the oven to 350°F (175°C). Prepare a 9-inch (23-cm) bundt pan by buttering all surfaces and dusting with a little flour to prevent sticking.

In a small pot, heat the brandy and raisins. Remove from the heat and let sit until the raisins soak up the brandy.

In a large pot, boil the whole potatoes for about 35–40 minutes until fork-tender. While still warm, peel off the skins and press the potatoes through a potato ricer into a large bowl. Set aside.

With an electric mixer, whip the egg whites and sugar to form firm peaks. Chill.

Combine the raisins, potatoes, egg yolks, and salt, carefully folding the ingredients until mixed. Chill to room temperature, then fold in the egg whites. Pour the batter into the prepared pan and bake for 20–30 minutes. Be sure a toothpick or wooden skewer comes out clean when plunged into the center of the cake. If it doesn't, bake a little longer and recheck. Allow to cool for 5–10 minutes and then flip out onto a metal cake rack or serving dish to finish cooling.

Olaf's Tip: As with most baking, accuracy is important, so weigh the potatoes. You must also steam them with their skin on as it helps to keep the potato starches in the potato. It is those starches that are the binding agent for the cake.

Part 2: Caramelized Almonds and Dates

1 cup	sugar	240 mL
1 cup	corn syrup	240 mL
¼ tsp.	cinnamon	1.2 mL
¼ cup	35% cream	60 mL
½ cup	cold unsalted butter, cubed	120 mL
1 cup	whole, peeled almonds	240 mL
1 cup	seeded and chopped dates	240 mL

In a small pot over medium heat, carefully melt the sugar until it caramelizes. Add the corn syrup, cinnamon, and cream. Remove from the heat and whisk in the cold butter cubes and fold in the almonds and dates. Warm when ready to serve.

Presentation: Place a wedge of the cake onto a plate and spoon a heaping tablespoon of the date compote on the side. A little scoop of vanilla ice cream couldn't hurt either!

"Spaghetti and Meatballs"

Serves 4

Everyone loves spaghetti and meatballs, but for dessert, you ask? At our Spezzo Restaurant in Richmond Hill, Ontario, kids and adults alike enjoy this fun and imaginative treat made with crepe "noodles," raspberry "sauce," chocolate "meatballs," kiwi "green peppers," and white chocolate "cheese"!

Part 1: "Spaghetti"

| ½ recipe | Crepe Batter (page 35) | ½ recipe |
| 3 cups | vanilla ice cream | 720 mL |

For the "spaghetti," make half the crepe recipe and cut the prepared crepes into ¼-inch (.6-cm) strips. Set aside in the refrigerator. When you are ready to assemble, you will be pressing the ice cream through a potato ricer. See Presentation.

Part 2: "Meatballs"

2 cups	35% cream	480 mL
1 lb.	semi-sweet chocolate chunks	455 g
1 cup	cocoa powder for dusting	240 mL

In a small pot, gently heat the cream. When simmering, whisk in the chocolate chunks. Pour into a bowl, cover, and chill for an hour. Once the mixture has set, using a melon baller or tablespoon, scoop out small balls and roll them around in the cocoa powder to cover. Chill.

Part 3: "Spaghetti Sauce"

½ cup	sugar	120 mL
1 cup	water	240 mL
4 cups	raspberries	960 mL

In a small pot, simmer the sugar and water to a syrup-like consistency. Add the raspberries and simmer for 5 minutes. Purée in a food processor, blender, or with a hand blender, then strain through a sieve. Chill.

Part 4: "The Cheese"

½ cup	grated white chocolate	120 mL

Part 5: "Diced Green Peppers"

2	kiwis, peeled and diced	2

Presentation: Into chilled pasta bowls or similar dishes, mound the "spaghetti" crepe strips and press the vanilla ice cream through a potato ricer to look like spaghetti. Top with the "spaghetti sauce" and place a few "meatballs" on top. Finally, top with some "cheese" and "green peppers."

Marzipan Creme Mousse with Bishop's Sauce

Serves 4

Marzipan's nutty flavors combined with a creamy mousse and the richness of red wine and fruit make this a fascinating dessert. Do we dare to suggest that it replace plum pudding at holiday dinners? Bishop's Sauce is a variation of mulled wine, a northern European drink that is made of warmed red wine, spices and orange peel.

Part 1: Marzipan Creme

5	sheets gelatin*	5
1½ cups	whole milk	360 mL
¼ cup	sugar	60 mL
1	vanilla bean, split and scraped	1
5 oz.	marzipan	140 g
1¼ cups	35% cream, whipped	300 mL
3 oz.	amaretto liqueur	85 mL

*See Glossary, page 202.

Dissolve the gelatin sheets in enough cold water to cover. Set aside. In a small pot, simmer the milk, sugar, and vanilla bean marrow. Stir in the marzipan until it dissolves. Add the drained gelatin sheets and simmer until everything is melted. Pour into a clean bowl through a fine metal sieve and chill to room temperature. Stir in the liqueur and fold in the whipped cream. Pour into parfait-style glasses or a plastic-lined mold or dish, for example, coffee cups or muffin pans, and chill for 2 hours. If using glasses, make sure they are big enough to fill half with mousse and half with the Bishop's Sauce, along with the fruit garnish.

Part 2: Bishop's Sauce

¾ cup	red wine	180 mL
¾ cup	orange juice	180 mL
1	orange, zest and juice of	1
⅓ cup	sugar	80 mL
½	cinnamon stick	½
2 Tbsp.	arrowroot powder or cornstarch	30 mL
1 cup	water	240 mL

Over medium heat in a medium-size pot, add the red wine, orange juice, zest, sugar, and cinnamon stick and simmer for 5 minutes or until it reaches a syrup-like consistency. Mix the arrowroot or cornstarch and water and add to the mixture, stirring until it thickens. Strain through a fine sieve and refrigerate until ready to serve.

Part 3: Garnish

¼ cup	toasted almond slices	60 mL
1 cup	pitted cherries, frozen or canned, drained	240 mL
1	orange, peeled, in segments	1

Presentation: If you opted to use a mold of some kind, pop the mousse out and remove the plastic wrap. Place on a pool of Bishop's Sauce and garnish with the almond slices, cherries, and oranges.

Glossary

al dente	to cook until almost tender but to leave some texture or bite of crispness.
blanching	to cook in boiling salt water for minutes and quickly transfer to ice water to stop the cooking process in order to maintain the color and flavor.
chiffonade	to roll vegetable or herb leaves and finely slice them into strips.
clarified butter	to slowly simmer unsalted butter until the water has evaporated and the milk solids, which sink to the bottom, leave the golden, clarified liquid on the surface.
confit	a French word meaning to salt the product and cook it slowly in its own fats/juices to preserve the quality of flavor.
deglaze	to add liquid to a pan to remove any flavor particles that have set themselves firm on the bottom of the pan.
dice	cut into small cubes, about $\frac{1}{2}$-inch (1.2 cm).
double-smoked bacon	same cut of pork as regular bacon, but it is double-smoked and aged—very flavorful and leaves next to no fat in the pan. The hard thick rind should be cut away.
fresh bread crumbs	make by taking stale white bread, removing the crust and pulsing in a blender/food processor to produce white, fluffy, absorbent crumbs.
gelatin sheets	brittle, plastic-like sheets, available at any grocery store, that act as a thickening agent for jelly, mousse or foams. One gelatin sheet is equal to $1\frac{1}{2}$ teaspoons of powered gelatin.
internal temperature	the temperature in the very center of the protein (meat), taken with a meat thermometer.
julienne	cut into match-stick strips.
kosher salt	an additive-free, coarse-grain salt that adds a distinct flavor and texture.
mandolin	a very sharp slicing device used to slice, julienne, make french fries, or waffle-cut.
mince	chop very finely.
mussels, cultivated	farm-raised in a controlled environment.

nuts or seeds, toasted	in a dry frying pan over medium heat, toss any type of nut until golden brown.
nutty brown butter	make by melting unsalted butter until it foams white, then keep cooking until it turns brown but just before it turns black.
ovenproof frying pan	any pan that can take the heat of the oven, especially the handle.
proofing dough	when working with yeast, when all the ingredients are put together, the dough is given time to rest until it swells to double its size to make sure the yeast is working.
quark	a European fresh cheese similar to fine ricotta or cream cheese.
reducing	to slowly simmer a stock or sauce to evaporate the water and leave concentrated flavors.
ribbons	when whisking an egg–sugar mixture, long strands (ribbons) should fall from the whisk into the batter when you hold the whisk up.
roasting	slow baking from all sides until natural sugars brown the food.
sabayon	a dessert made with egg yolks, wine, and sugar whisked into a custard.
sauté	quickly cooking and tenderizing foods in hot oil.
sear	to form a crusty brown surface on meat or fish to lock in the juices.
strips	slightly thicker than julienne.
sweating	cook on low heat until translucent.
temper	to bring two ingredients close to the same temperature so that the ingredients are not shocking each other as they mix.
vanilla bean	a long, thin black pod that you cut in half lengthwise, then scrape out the vanilla marrow or seeds—can be substituted with 1/2 tsp. (2.5 mL) pure vanilla extract.
wilting	quickly heating foods in a hot pan to reduce the natural moisture content, then removing from the pan.

Index